WORTH ANOTHER TRY

Pursuant Endless Grace

By
Gregory S. Faust

Copyright © 2015 by Gregory S. Faust

Worth Another Try
Pursuant Endless Grace
by Gregory S. Faust

Printed in the United States of America.

Edited by Xulon Press

ISBN 9781498455459

All rights reserved solely by the author. The author guarantees all contents are original and do not infringe upon the legal rights of any other person or work. No part of this book may be reproduced in any form without the permission of the author. The views expressed in this book are not necessarily those of the publisher.

Unless otherwise indicated, Scripture quotations are taken from the New International Version (NIV). Copyright © 1973, 1978, 1984, 2011 by Biblica, Inc.™. Used by permission. All rights reserved.

www.xulonpress.com

Worth Another Try

(PURSUANT ENDLESS GRACE)

The Lord is not slow in keeping his promise, as some understand slowness. Instead, he is patient with you, not wanting anyone to perish, but for everyone to come to repentance.

(II Peter 3:9)

The Lord said, "Cast your net on the other side of the boat and you will find some."

(John 21:6)

Table of Contents

Chapter 1: No Greater Value 9

Chapter 2: Ever Given It a Thought? 19

Chapter 3: Fairy Tales Forever? 28

    The Greek Olympians

    A View of the Titans

    Greek vs. Roman gods

    Relatively Minor Gods

    Hindu, Chinese, Mayan, Norse, and Egyptian Deities

Chapter 4: One More Try 53

    Why Keep Trying?

Chapter 5: Divine Mercy, a Reasonable Verdict! 62

Chapter 6: Without Excuse! 87

    Unconditional Love is Not Saving Grace!

Endless Resource!

Many Strong Resources!

Chapter 7: Is the Word of Grace Enough? 102

Chapter 8: The Final Question 113

Belief through Experience

Chapter 1

No Greater Value

What is anybody worth? Do you think there is ever a clear-cut answer to that question? There is one individual we can trust to always have a precise answer to that question. The only individual who consistently has the same answer for all of us is God. You can be certain you are worth everything He could ever give. Every one of us is viewed as valuable enough for a sacrifice, the gift of what God accomplished through redemption. We are worth the most profound sacrifice of one's own life.

There are many men and women who have accumulated millions and even billions of dollars, but how are they measured in worth? Each person is worth precisely the same value to our God as any king, pauper, thief, strumpet, or even murderer. It will serve us well to discover the love and truth that so many have ushered to the forefront of mankind by the power of the Holy Spirit. Our Holy Lord believes deeply in your worth.

Worth Another Try

I would say no matter who you are, you are always considered to be *worth another try*. No matter how often I try to convey the love of Christ and the truth of redemption through His wondrous gift, I know it is worth continuing. Regardless of the time spent to present the good news or even any feeling of rejection, I still find it to be worth another try. It is worth the opportunity to provide seeds to my beloved friends and family members so they can incontrovertibly consider the joy of eternal life or the consequence of not knowing absolute salvation. What would you say God is worth to you? Do you think He is worthy of knowing the unmistakable certainty which He offers us? He considers us very valuable; do you consider God worthy of absolute assurance? Being thought of as valuable is what we all seek, but determining value is an intricate process.

When compressed, coal becomes one of the most precious of objects: valuable diamonds. Most people would agree diamonds of are great value, even though they are basically just altered minerals. Another crystalline product that looks somewhat like diamonds is salt. Salt is worth so much to sustain human life; it preserves, flavors, and is even used as currency. Gold is a simple ore that could be just as useless and meaningless as unprocessed iron or just as barren, if it were not for the curing. The refining of the many types of gold requires such toil. Low-grade gold refinement requires a solution of cyanide, which is a well known poison. Refractory ore contains carbon and must be heated to over one thousand degrees, which removes sulfide and carbon. These processes are complex and can be dangerous. Yet to gain its worth, we humans still go the distance to get gold, which is an unequaled financial standard throughout the world. Some things need to be worked on to gain value.

Sculptures or portraits that take endless hours to commemorate some great person are worth millions. To portray heroes and form icons carved into a mountain, Mount Rushmore cost about $1,000,000 at the time it was made. The continued pursuit of this project by Gutzon Borglum and his son Lincoln extended from 1927 to 1941. A lifetime of effort, it seemed, and still, money was what stopped the final touches which had been planned. Michelangelo's David and the Sistine Chapel are also examples of value beyond reckoning. It is almost incalculable to determine the cost of all the world's graven images and portraits. The endless array of figures and images tells us memory is of great value.

What type of measurement will convey a person's viewpoint of worthiness? How is value measured? The average cost of a space mission is about $450,000,000 just to discover more about our surroundings. The Hubble space project itself, thus far, has been estimated at a cost approaching one billion dollars. What makes it worth that much? To replace critical parts of our human body is of enormous cost. Some estimates of the most expensive procedures that have been performed are: heart transplant—$778,700, bone marrow—$676,800, lung transplant—$657,800, intestine transplant—$1,121,800, liver transplant—$523,400, and many more that are astounding. I imagine the recipients of those were very glad that someone considered them to be worth another try. The current cost for an average terminal cancer patient to survive just an additional five years is over $30,000 to $40,000 per year. Who decides the balance of cost versus the value of the patient?

Do you consider yourself to be worth millions? The average doctor's salary in U.S. is upwards of $170,000, the estimates I find for lawyers range near $150,000 and higher, and these are excluding specialists in either field of practice. The mean average salary was $770,000 for a football player in the year 2010, but do we consider what a short career they have. The Pro basketball player's average salary can be anywhere from $3,000,000 to $5,000,000 a year. Tiger Woods made as much as ten million in salary earnings for 3 consecutive years. The contracts with Tiger outside and above event earnings are over $78,000,000 in total gross income in just one of his years as a professional. Some of the highest paid salaries for actors range between $9,000,000 and $24,000,000 per contract. Are these people worth this much? It seems if our bodies perform a task we consider needed or render a service, or even entertain, then our value can be staggering based on others' shared perception.

Astoundingly, our human body once it has been separated from the soul and spirit has been calculated to have a chemical value no higher than one hundred fifty dollars. It seems that when our loved ones are in dire straits, they are of extreme value. The Chilean people consider their loved ones worth an expense in the millions. The recent 2010 mining accident trapped thirty-three individuals, and the final cost of freedom was well over $33,000,000 in U.S. currency. So, I guess you could say most any person should be worth at least a million dollars.

To create the new born North American nation through revolution and gain freedom for her, we lost over 25,000 lives in combat or civil action. That is a staggering amount considering the population of the time and those willing to stand for freedom and be counted in the struggle. The overall loss of life to secure a united and separate nation was devastating, but freedom is worth the cost. Abraham Lincoln truly understood the value that each life represented and the price of freedom for our beloved brothers and sisters that once were enslaved in this country. The cost of freedom there was about 618,000 American lives. Some estimates show that the death toll for the Civil War was as high as 850,000. He felt that our nation's civil integrity and moral principles were worth this many lives even though no foreign antagonist was harassing the people. Human freedom is undoubtedly of great worth.

Later in our United States history, in 1941, we entered a foreign war. Many people in our country had bitter doubts about whether we should even get involved overseas. The value of human life without subversion was the dynamic that secured our loyalty. The merit of helping our allies in Europe to be delivered from the horrifying cloud of Nazism tallied a cost of over 291,000 lives, and some world war estimates reach over 405,000 American deaths.

With the definition of worth being so subjective, don't you find it peculiar that the grand designer of the universe, who is more glorious than any of our comprehension or appreciation, finds us to be of inestimable value? We are told in Scripture that the Lord is "long suffering" and patient that all would come to know His sacrifice (2 Peter 3:9). He is literally in pain, waiting and providing as many seeds as possible, even pouring them out to every person, through so many means of absorption that it should be profusely evident. You can see this definition described in the book of Romans, Chapter 1, verses 20 through 27. Be clear in knowing that God almighty, the creator of everything and the one in control of all final things, is worthy of trust. He is surely worthy of coming to know Him and discover how much he feels *you are worth to Him!* Just the way you are, you are worthy of the most perfect sacrifice ever conceived.

That is right; every one of us is valuable enough for His death on the cross. Some people believe this event can be taken lightly, but scripture describes the death God chose for His Son as the most horrifying and degrading demise anyone can experience. I am certain I could not describe the crucifixion more intricately than the Bible. It is safe to say this bloodletting, bashing, whipping, beard ripping, nail piercing, belittlement, betrayal, torture, and stabbing is by no means a way for a person to be treated, especially one without guilt. Yes, this kind of punishment was meant for a *thing*, a horrid and despicable thing, it was meant to crush the one thing that stands between us and a holy God. This sacrifice was meant for *sin*. Sin had to be smashed to remove the sting of death and make sin removable from mankind so that through His blood-filled sacrifice, we could all have redemption. The Torah (Old Testament) and the epistles (New Testament) clearly tell us there is *no forgiveness and no cleansing without the shedding of blood* (Leviticus 17:11, Hebrews 9:21–22).

Perfect and eternal cleansing is only possible by the only *one* who demands it. That "one" who is, or ever could be, worthy of a life sacrifice to purge sin for all humankind. Only "God with us," Emanuel, Elohim, Jehovah, could have the supernatural power and worthiness to carry the punishment of all mankind and have sin demolished by his blood. Yes, God in heaven finds us of enough importance to redeem us through death and resurrection of the one and to wash us from all our sins.

God considers you of value enough to die for you. How worthy do you consider God? Worthy of simple curiosity, minor interest, barroom banter, intelligent discussion, singularity, or of hope? Maybe you suppose God is actually worthy of love. If so, how do you show love for someone who was willing to take punishment where no payment of His own was owed, someone who was willing to feel the bitter incomparable pain of separation, destruction, devastation of sin hung upon himself? We are of such great value to God that we were *worth another try*. God gave us himself in person! He did not show up in dozens of forms, or confuse us with multiple ways to *gain* some prize, or even give us a best practice lesson by any person or prophet; he came amongst us in person for one reason. He came to crush sin and redeem us *if we would accept and believe*.

Someone who was talking to me recently asked about the difference between Christianity and all other religions. We had discussed this many times. I felt the answer I gave would probably be lost in the emptiness of relativism or even be dismissed but I felt God never gives up and neither should I. I am sure this soul is worth another try. I was truthfully so glad he asked, so I explained once again, "Every man made religion is about making oneself 'worthy,' or making ourselves good enough." But Christ is not that, He did not come to make bad people good, he came to make *dead* people *alive*.

The Holy Spirit had unquestionably conducted me. I was able to clearly say…."All religions are from man! Christ is the solution from God." This is the good news of the Gospel of Jesus Christ and the difference between personal relationships with God, through the Son, versus a man made way that pursues *being good enough* for a perfect God. It is entirely unreasonable to reject the gift of eternal life. If God finds you infinitely valuable, don't you want to have a rational way to respond?

It seems very rational, that when the Holy of Holies transcended the boundaries of time and space and placed himself in the role of "a guilt-filled sinner" and took on an untold amount of punishment and finally death, he did not do that to distinguish a bargaining chip or down payment. Rather, the Bible tells us his words were, "*It is finished!*" (John 19:30).

This was a term during Christ's time about payment of debt to mean "*All debt is paid.*" He did not ask for something; instead he did it for every person who would ever come into being on this earth, irrespective of any degree of wrongdoing, so even the most horrid of sins can be relinquished. Do you understand what that means? It means our names are written in the lamb's book of Eternal life by the truth of the cross, if we choose salvation by grace. It means the choice is ours to freely receive it gladly or reject Him in place of the bombastic nature of our own merit.

Through Christ we can be born again and see the kingdom of God. How many times must a person hear that very same thing before they personalize it and wonder "does this mean me?" Unless you are a believer, why have you not taken this personally? Take it personally! You must be born again, and this means every person, or you shall never see the Kingdom of God. How much more plain can that be?

I ask, are you born again? Do you know what it means? It means everyone is worth another try and can be redeemed on God's terms. Here is what the Holy Bible reveals: it distinctly states that you must be born again, *or else!* (John 3:3–6). That "*or else*" consequence is to never see the kingdom of God. When Christ explained this to the great Hebrew teacher Nicodemus, he went on to plainly say that you must be born of the Spirit. That is the Spirit of believing (faith) in the salvation of the cross, not our own deeds. The Gospel of John proceeds to tell us in verse 3:18, "Whoever believes in Him is not condemned, but whoever has not believed is condemned already, because they have not believed in the name of the only Son of God."

To engage this Gospel truth, repent, and know salvation, is not a complex change at all; instead, it is simple and eternal. It is a spiritual awakening and a one hundred and eighty-degree turn from our own work-based belief, to instead receive the gift of grace "alone" through Jesus, as the only authentic way to heaven.

We should make our reaction to the creator, the one who values us so much, be a response of peace. If we never receive the Savior, we will *remain dead in our sins.* No man made ideas or deeds can remove our sin. Only the Son of God can remove sin, and we all have fallen short of God's glory (Rom 3:23–24). If you want to be born again, let your yes be yes *or* your no be no! Reflect on this, and you will discover that your response can be confident acknowledgement and grateful reception, or it can be rejection and continued doubt unto woeful loss.

God has proven that we are worth another try. We should be excited about the chance of gaining everlasting joy that is available through the gift of grace and being viewed by God as *having no greater value*. Being of such great importance and embracing the truth, is not just a foolhardy or quaint colloquialism, but instead *grace* is the truth, and the truth will set you free.

Chapter 2

Ever Given It a Thought?

The idea of time passing away and not getting the full use of the minutes or the loss of anything you can never retrieve is truly a debilitating notion. Yet there are other times when we crave peaceful reflection, blissful ignorance, or down right exhilaration and joy in letting go and doing nothing whatsoever. Time is an essence or element that is non-refundable and irretrievable once it has been lost. For instance, just run this concept of time being "lost" by a person who has been in traffic for a seemingly endless period of moving nowhere. Or in retrospect, quiz someone who was in just the right place, at just the right time! It is the most precious commodity we have, and therefore it is the most fraught with peril if mistreated.

I know a very close friend whose daughter was a devoted fanatic about timeliness. She was virtually never late and always made ample arrangements or sensible decisions to be right on time. It was even a bone of contention with her family and friends sometimes and was perceived as an annoying trait because some of them felt they could not live up to her expectations.

One bright sunny autumn morning, she was preparing to be interviewed for a new job, one which she had sought for a very long time. She knew that she was a shoe-in for the position, if only she could just interview and communicate with the company executives. However, she was confounded at every turn of events which went awry on this incredibly brilliant morning where nothing could have been, should have been, or was going to be wrong. There was such a beautiful sky and she had such a positive goal to achieve. How could anything be amiss? Yet a mystery remained. There were bathroom troubles, the car, and her final household hurdle, but alas, she still made it to the railway on time, just barely. She was praying heartily to have these inconceivable impositions cease.

Maybe this torrent of problems was going to be averted after all, it seemed. The train into the city was almost running right on time. She had planned ahead and knew the schedule of each ride that she would need to catch to get her to the meeting. Although she had been delayed by unforeseen things she had planned ahead by knowing the times of every conceivable circumstance, so she got out of the train into the station ready to get another ride, it was the latest of each planned ride, but maybe it was going to be just fine. She was headed to her interview and only needed to step out of the railcar and scurry up the stairs to meet with the people to have her dream come true. A quick glance at her watch confirmed that the choice of transportation had been the right one and that the previously scrutinized travel times to keep her ahead of schedule were going to be rewarded. Also, the choice of this last lap of transportation now was moving even better than usual. Things were running very tight but not yet late. Even at 8:50 am she was no more than minutes away from the start of a life long career opportunity. In her eyes, this September day was going to be a monumental day for celebration.

Then came the most infuriating sound anyone could ever hear when traveling on a railway car: a subway car, to be exact. It was a conductor's voice interrupting the serenity of knowing you had mastered the travel schedule and it was going to be OK. It was muffled, and somewhat confusing. It sounded like he said there was smoke, but not a fire, in the station where they were scheduled to stop, so they were traveling past it, to let off everyone at the next one.

That was fine; she knew her environment and knew the city map and hoped she could run up the stairs, then back down the street and straight up the elevator. She could still make an appearance, though it might be, for the first time ever, a *slightly late* appearance. She had to accept it, but she could not help but think, "Lord, how could so many things go bad? Why would this happen?" She got off quickly, bolted out, raced off the subway, and headed up the stairs. The people around her seemed to be just a blur and a buzz. Many were muttering, and some even seemed aghast at something. She did not have time for that right now; to listen or be interested was not an option. The stairs were clear, and she was going to fly right up them. She was moving and determined to get there as fast as possible, even though she was now certainly late; it was 9:02 am.

Arriving at the top of the stairs of the subway and still a bit frazzled from her apparent failure, she suddenly paused and was sent staggering backwards because of a high-pitched, incredibly loud sound from above. This was an uncommon thing to hear in the inner city ... it sounded and felt like the colossal roar of a plane engine, and then—! Yes, it was just what you might have guessed: the percussion of a screaming fuselage exploding through steel and glass. It was inexplicable.

In all the subsequent attempts to describe the ordeal to her Dad, she was never quite able to describe or revisit mentally the actual scene and impact of Flight 175 crashing into the South Tower of the World Trade Center. It blasted into the tower at 590 miles per hour. It was thunderous! It caused everyone to flinch, cringe, and scurry simultaneously, like dogs that have been beaten endlessly, hearing the ogre sound of the assailant. It was piercing, devastating, horrifying! Then the most grotesque feeling of all swarmed her belly and strangled her throat. "Oh Dear Lord; I was supposed to be there and in the meeting, and yet I was late."

Her thoughts assembled quickly, and she realized the meeting was to have been up *there,* way up there, and to be ... in the upper floors. She was wise enough to move away to a safe distance as the rest of this travesty unraveled, having already suffered eye and tissue damage from the horrific cloud of debris. Her later calculations in the following weeks to come, in the safety of her home, confirmed what she had felt then. Prompt timing uninterrupted, just as she had planned, would have placed her "early" and directly in the middle of the unthinkable destruction.

That day, the realization of such destructive timing and associated endless despair, had occurred for thousands of people. That day a miracle of *time* or timing had also occurred for many other thousands of people. That day many thousands were spared the horror of a monster's plan. For many others that day, time stood still, and heartbreak was all that lingered!

For the first time ever, my friend's daughter had been delayed, and it seems quite clear it was no mistake. God was in control, and she had been spared.

Time is irreplaceable, so I now come to my point having prefaced this chapter with a viewpoint of what time can mean for many people and what it should mean to all of us. It should be viewed as precious when evaluating our position with respect to the supernatural or eternal. The irrefutable fact is that we all die and pass away. We have a visible end to life as we know it in this natural world. Yet do we spend sufficient time, any time, or suitable time in the pursuit of answers and the absolute revelation of what God is, or might be, or what he expects from us? Do we consider what is He all about? Have you ever spent truly concerted time to think about it?

Rather than try to share the most common ideas of the masses, which supposedly emerges from time spent to discover supernatural eternal truths, I will let you in on the secret. Certainty, assurance, and everlasting life are not gained by time or effort or even greater knowledge or universal understanding. "Although the world *through its wisdom* did not know Him; God was pleased through the foolishness of what was preached to save those who believe" (I Corinthians 1:21). Eternal answers are received by the simple trust and faith that truth and grace are *timeless*.

I have heard answers from hundreds of people, and it puzzles me to see how most people have not spent an exhaustive amount of time to examine the thought of the end of one's own self. What I have discovered is that they have entrusted that idea of good, bad, permanence, and the judgment of God to local hearsay or traditional theories. Each person seems to have an opinion without having spent much time on the subject. More surprisingly, when I seek any debate, they cannot convey a simple assessment of what they think would make any of us good enough, to stand before a perfect, everlasting, holy God, and then tell Him that He *owes* us something. How much time have you spent on the eternal question? Have you ever given it a thought?

The most remedial inquiry used to examine merit is one based on "goodness" versus "badness" and a simple examination of the root of good and evil. Everyone seems to want to compare this issue to a norm; they want to believe they are good enough. Most pointedly, I have found when I ask someone, "do you believe you should go to heaven when you die," I can guarantee that answer would be based on their own measurement of worthiness compared to an average or something resembling a balance of good and evil. This comes from the common subterfuge known as relativism, which means "how good I am compared to someone else, or the human average." This comparative reasoning is an association of morality which is a linear or lateral relationship towards one another, versus spirituality, which is supernatural or singular vertical relationship. To assess our own deeds in a relationship with God as a measurement for virtue is obtuse to say the least.

Time is the best gift you were ever given to use for understanding the simplest of notions. Time is a measurement, not a physical substance; thus, you have been given all the days you will ever need to make an everlasting decision. Every person will have no excuse when they face the fact of an eternal afterlife. If a person has seen the glory of God and not responded, it will be crushing, because they have been given a sensible or reasonable amount of time to know the eternal answer for certain. Thus, they will be held accountable (Rom 1:20–28). Also, if a person has believed that we are just dust and returning to said same, it will not prevent a face to face meeting with God if they are wrong. To abandon the gift of the Holy Sprit and ignore the necessity of cohesion to our creator is unforgivable (Matt 12:31–32). We all have time, and we can surely see how catastrophic it can be to be in the wrong place at the wrong time. Our eternal destiny is worth every second, minute, hour, or day to reach the true conclusion.

Vagueness will result in destruction. When Lot's wife turned to see the destruction of Sodom and Gomorrah, it was out of vague trust and desire to live without the precision of God's truth. She was not considering a former lifetime lost; rather, she was concluding that the future God offered was not going to be as good. If we trust in comfort alone, we are doomed. Split-second timing of the heart is known by God. Her loss was because of a determined heart of continual indecision. I'll tell you; If I had been escorted away from a tragedy by "angels," I would trust the future that God had in store for me. I would receive the straightforwardness of a *gift* when it is so simple (I Corinthians 1:21).

In your lifetime, you will most likely be confronted by friends, family, coworkers, or acquaintances who want to discuss with you, reveal, or explain a religion, dogmatism, faith, or afterlife discourse. I would beseech you to listen to all of the man-made concepts if you wish, but I would implore you to take the *time* to compare them to the *one* completely different idea. Listen carefully to the idea which embodies simplicity, credence, and worshipful honor to be given to the one who provides the everlasting answer. Give yourself time to learn the Gospel. The word means Good News ... isn't it time for you to know all there is to know about the Gospel of Christ our Savior. Have you ever given it a thought?

If you give the Gospel due time and you contritely see the need for redemption by perfect cleansing. When you conclude that the mercy of God's own Son is the only perfect sacrifice. Then you will have given it a thought and reached an eternal blessing of time well spent. If you are willing to receive that simple truth that grace is salvation forever, rather than untimely work-based gimmicks, or myth-filled prescriptions, then your afterlife will be lived wonderfully beyond comprehension.

Have you given it a thought? For the Word of the Lord proclaims, "No eye has seen, no ear has heard, no mind has conceived, the glory God has prepared for those who love him" (I Corinthians 2:9).

Chapter 3

Fairy Tales Forever?

Worldwide, we have a more sundry belief system and an *expanding* viewpoint that it is possible for a *single God* to exist, yet he would choose to reveal himself in an endless array of names, concepts, and haphazard methods of communication. Incredibly, all of these ways are contradictory in nature, deity, symbolism, and above all, pathology to intimacy or means of redemption. This hypothesis could only amount to confusion of purpose and lack of potency in our relationship to an almighty God. Of course, there is also the endless turmoil of fighting amongst ourselves about whose god is best.

Failures to understand the truth over thousands of years in which the earth's inhabitants have embraced myth have not seemed to prevent the continuation of error and the endless influx of misguidance. Even within our civilized and educated nations, there is tremendous deprivation of truth. Let me ask you, what emotion or feeling you experience when you examine the astonishing magnitude and impact of myths throughout the existence of mankind? I know that I cannot help but feel intrigue, puzzlement, frustration, grief, and sometimes even distress. Mostly, I feel embarrassed for the supposed elite, educated, academia, intelligent, or so-called cultured thinkers of our era. Can we claim true enlightenment when we exemplify such continuing failure of cohesion, peace, and compatibility, and still we remain so veritably *lost?*

To believe we can achieve wholeness and diversity through myth is by no means a proper way to secure social or spiritual oneness or solidarity for humankind. Otherwise, the important intangible factors of security, commonality, and brotherhood encapsulated in the actual truth, would be lost to every orator's whim or passing fancy. Why would a single *God* so utterly confuse the people he supposedly loves with such horrible inconsistencies and contradictions throughout all of recorded history? He would not! It is far more reasonable to adopt the truth that is found in the Bible? "For *God is not the author of confusion,* but of peace, as in all churches of the saints" (1 Corinthians 14:33). The one true God is not a pocket full of myths designed to test us or arbitrarily instruct mankind, rather God is a supernatural being of perfection, filled with holiness, love, and also grace towards an unholy sinful race of humans.

The following mythological journey that I want to take you on is an attempt to unveil the preposterous theories, which, to be equitable, must include *all* of the gods out there. Unlike many things in our lives, when claiming to seek truth about

God there is no road in between. You must choose! There is no gray area, you are either seeking the incontestable, incontrovertible truth or you are willing to embrace the amazing *bulk* of errant confusion that is considered international oneness or interplanetary melding or continuous interstellar spirit fusion. Let's face it! There is actually only *"One True God,"* or there are hundreds of thousands of deities! So, maybe you can make your own declaration after browsing this incredibly meager collection of examples!

These limited selections of myth will bear some familiarity to many people in the world today. Even within the nations and countries of their origin they are now considered myth when once they were perceived as truth. Review the names and descriptions of this small sample that history proves were viewed as real yet now have passed away as myth or are not considered today as a form of deity. It just doesn't seem fair to these debunked gods. Why do we choose to neglect them now? Some gods in these selections are still worshiped in Asia, India, Australia, Africa, remote islands, South and Central America, some parts of the U.S. and many, many other places, even though all of science has proven the spiritual claims and associated creation theories of these false gods to be completely impossible.

To display perspective to my anxiety over the lack of absolute truth seeking, I have selected a minuscule amount of deity names and descriptions that are undoubtedly now viewed as myth in our world today. Yet the concept of polytheism is still embraced as *fact* by many who incorporate it into their perception today. Hence, choosing the top seven or ten to worship or any number that excludes *all* of them is not practical or possible. To deviate from including all gods is not an option. The belief in randomness or multi-gods has even permeated a once sound and stable union of people, the United States of America. So, I ask, is there a pageant of beings called gods, or is there really just one God?

Rather than provide a massive history lesson, I would implore you to see the necessity of considering these myths real gods if we are to regard multiple gods as truth. They would surely need to be understood in great detail if we choose the apparent current theory of polytheism. The choice of Greek notables and descriptions should be familiar to anyone from the Western culture. There are even some historians that claim that Greek mythology is the basis of Western philosophy and culture in the modern world today. As a convincing example, I would invite you to see what mythical creatures we would need to continue to embrace if polytheism is to be viewed as truthful!

The Greek Olympians (a limited description)

- **Zeus:** Zeus overthrew his Father Cronus, then drew lots with his brothers Poseidon and Hades, won the draw and became the supreme ruler. He is lord of the sky, the rain god. He hurls thunderbolts at those who displease

him. He is married to Hera, and yet he is famous for his many affairs.
- **Poseidon:** Poseidon is the brother of Zeus. During the drawing of lots when Cronus was overthrown, he drew lots with Zeus and Hades for shares of the world. His prize was lord of the sea. He was worshiped by seamen. His weapon, a trident, can shake and shatter any object. He is second only to Zeus and believed to have made the first horse after many failures. He is quarrelsome and greedy, as one can see in his many attempts to take over cities ruled by other gods.
- **Hades:** Another brother of Zeus had the worst draw and was made lord of the underworld, ruling over the dead. Hades rarely leaves the underworld. He is unpitying and terrible, but not capricious. His wife is Persephone, whom he abducted. He is the King of the dead, but death itself is another god, Thanatos.
- **Hera:** Zeus's wife and sister. Raised by the Titans Ocean and Tethys. She is the protector of marriage and care of married women. Hera's marriage was founded in strife with Zeus, who courted her unsuccessfully, so he turned to trickery and changed himself into a disheveled cuckoo. Hera felt sorry for the bird and held it to her breast, at which point Zeus resumed normal form, and, taking advantage of the surprise, raped her.
- **Hestia:** Zeus's sister, a virgin goddess. She is the goddess of the Hearth, the symbol of the house around

which a new born child is carried before it is received into the family. Each city had a public hearth sacred to Hestia, where the fire was never allowed to go out.

- **Ares:** Son of Zeus and Hera. He was disliked by both parents. He is the god of war, considered murderous and bloodstained and yet a coward.
- **Athena:** Daughter of Zeus, who sprang full grown in armor from his forehead, and thus has no mother. She was Zeus's favorite child and was allowed to use his weapons, including his thunderbolt. The owl is her favorite bird. She is also a virgin goddess.
- **Apollo** Apollo is the son of Zeus and Leto. His twin sister is Artemis. He is the god of music, playing a golden lyre. The Archer, far shooting with a silver bow. The god who taught man medicine. The god of truth, who cannot speak a lie. One of Apollo's more important daily tasks is to harness his chariot with four horses and drive the Sun across the sky. The god of light. He is famous for his oracle at Delphi.
- **Aphrodite** Aphrodite is the goddess of love, desire, and beauty. In addition to her natural gifts, she has a magical girdle that compels anyone she wishes to desire her. There are two accounts of her birth. One says she is the daughter of Zeus and Dione. The other goes back to when Cronus castrated Uranus and tossed his severed genitals into the sea. Aphrodite then arose from the sea foam on a giant scallop and walked to shore in Cyprus.

She is the wife of Hephaestus. The myrtle is her tree. The dove, the swan, and the sparrow her birds.
- **Hermes** Hermes is the son of Zeus and Maia. He is Zeus's messenger. He is the fastest of the gods. He wears winged sandals, a winged hat, and carries a magic wand. He is the god of thieves and god of commerce. He is the guide for the dead to go to the underworld. He invented the lyre, the pipes, the musical scale, astronomy, weights and measures, boxing, gymnastics, and the care of olive trees.
- **Artemis** Artemis is the daughter of Zeus and Leto. Her twin brother is Apollo. Like Apollo, she hunts with silver arrows. She became associated with the moon. She is a virgin goddess of chastity. She also presides over childbirth, which may seem odd for a virgin, but goes back to causing Leto no pain when she was born. She became associated with Hecate.
- **Hephaestus** Hephaestus is the son of Zeus and Hera. Sometimes it is said that Hera alone produced him and that he has no father. He is the only god to be physically ugly. He is also lame. Accounts as to how he became lame vary. Some say that Hera, upset by having an ugly child, flung him from Mount Olympus into the sea, breaking his legs. Others say that he took Hera's side in an argument with Zeus, and Zeus flung him off Mount Olympus. He is the god of fire and the forge. He is the smith and armor master of the gods. He uses a

volcano as his forge. He is the patron god of both smiths and weavers, and is kind and peace-loving. His wife is Aphrodite.

Short Descriptions of the Titans (earth gods)

Uranus: Uranus is the sky god and supposed *first ruler*. He is the son of Gaea, who *created him without a mate*. He then became the husband of Gaea, and together they had many offspring, including twelve of the Titans.

Gaea: Gaea is the Earth goddess. She mated with her son Uranus to produce the remaining Titans. Gaea started as a Neolithic earth-mother worshipped before the Indo-European invasion that eventually led to the Hellenistic civilization.

Cronus: Cronus was the ruling Titan who came to power by castrating his father, Uranus. His wife was Rhea. Their offspring were the first of the Olympians.

Rhea: Rhea was the wife of Cronus.

Mnemosyne: Mnemosyne was the Titan of memory and mother of the muses.

Prometheus: Prometheus was the wisest Titan. He was the son of Iapetus. When Zeus revolted against Cronus, Prometheus deserted the other Titans and fought on Zeus's side. His name means "forethought," and he was able to foretell the future. He gave mankind the gift of fire. He was to be left there for all eternity or until he agreed to work against the plot to overthrow Zeus and expose the children who wanted to replace him. He was eventually rescued by Heracles.

Iapetus: Iapetus was the father of Prometheus, Epimetheus, Menoetius, and Atlas by Clymene.

Coeus: Coeus is the Titan of Intelligence. Father of Leto.

Phoebe: Phoebe is the Titan of the Moon. Mother of Leto.

Tethys: Tethys is the wife of Oceanus.

Epimetheus: Epimetheus was an idiot Titan; his name means "afterthought." He also accepted the gift of Pandora from Zeus, which lead to the introduction of evil into the world. Nice move.

Atlas: Atlas was the son of Iapetus. Unlike his brothers Prometheus and Epimetheus, Atlas fought with the other Titans, supporting Cronus against Zeus.

Dione: Dione is, according to Homer in the Iliad, the mother of Aphrodite.

Themis: Themis was the Titan of justice and order.

This type of list and review is probably tedious enough for anyone, so I have not included many of the hundreds of descriptions. However, I wanted to include one of the most prominent cultures in history, and those mythical gods that were just as profound in ancient Rome as they were in ancient history and in many other cultures. The Roman gods are as much a collection of modified gods from other cultures as they are unique to the Roman society itself. The following is a composite of the most common Roman deities and the Greek counterpart and likeness of that major Roman god.

Greek vs. *Roman gods*

- Aphrodite=Venus
- Ares=Mars
- Athena=Minerva
- Demeter=Ceres
- Hades=Pluto
- Hephaistos=Vulcan
- Hermes=Mercury
- Hestia=Vesta
- Cronos=Saturn
- Persephone=Proserpina
- Poseidon=Neptune
- Zeus=Jupiter

Relatively minor Greek / Roman gods

- Erinyes=Furiae
- Eris=Discordia
- Eros=Cupid
- Fates=Morae
- Graces=Charities
- Helios=Sol
- Horus=Horae
- Pan=Faunus
- Tyche=Fortuna

The list of entries in the history and fiction books is never-ending, but I hope my point of inclusion or exclusion is understood. If we are to abandon the *one* true God for any of these false gods, then *all* of them must be honored and embraced.

The next group actually includes some current day and past historical figures of myth and names that still have some following and a basis for misunderstanding true theology. If you visit India today, you may find over 320 million verifiable names or gods that are worshiped or given credence. An attempt to call them conceptual or concepts still does not decrease the confusion, as they are surely called gods. This is a limited example of names and the theoretical characteristics of these gods. You may choose to breeze through the list and descriptions, but understand that many people still show them faith or consideration.

Hindu gods / India

Aditi: Mother of the gods. Ruler of the sky, earth, past, and future.

Agni: The Fire god. Three flaming heads, three legs and seven arms. Ruler of weather. *Aryaman:* god of the Heavens. Ruler of the sun, moon, winds, waters, and seasons. Sounds much like the last one.

Asvins: Known also as twins or Nasatyas. Gods of the morning rode in their gold car drawn by horses or birds. Physician gods. Rulers of the morning, evening stars, healing, old age, and the protection of love and marriage.

Brahma: Part of the triad with Vishnu and Shiva. Father of the gods, men, and the world. Guardian of the world, riding a swan, he has red skin, four heads, and white robes. He also has four arms in which he carries his scepter, Vedas, a bow, and a water jug. Ruler of wisdom, knowledge, and Magic.

Brihaspati: Master of magic power and the priesthood. Ruler of Magic, priesthood, and created beings.

Buddha: The divine teacher. An avatar/incarnation of **Vishnu the god.** Ruler of Spiritual illumination, wisdom, and of course *self-realization* (which cannot bring humans closer to god, unless we are a god also).

Chandra: The Moon god whose name is derived from the intoxicating, hallucinogenic swill made for the gods. Ruler of psychic visions and dreams, rising on the inner planes, and pleasant forgetfulness.

Devi: Also known as "Shakti." Shiva's Consort. Most powerful of the goddesses.

Durga: One of the triad, along with the goddesses Uma and Parvati. In her aspect of Durga Pratyangira, she is a yellow woman with ten arms who carries a trident, sword, drum, and bowl of blood. Mother goddess. Rules over death, destruction, futility, ruin, comfort, help, power, nurturing, protection, and defense.

Gandharvas: Gods of the air, rain clouds and rain. Rulers of truths, medicines, musical skills, air, clouds, and rain.

Ganesha: Elephant-headed god *of scribes* and merchants. Ruler of good luck, literature, books, and writing.

Ganga: Goddess of the river Ganges and responsible for purification.

Gauri: Benign aspect of the great goddess. Ruler of good fortune.

Indra: King of the gods, and guardian of the Eastern quarter. Fair hair with golden skin riding a horse, elephant (Airavata), or a chariot drawn by two tawny horses. Ruler of war, weather, fertility, sky, warriors, violence, weather, fertility, lightning, reincarnation, rain, strength, bravery, horses, elephants, love, sensual desire, rainbow, personal intervention, law, magic power, rivers, time, and seasons.

Jyestha: Goddess of bad luck. Rules over revenge and dark magic.

Kali Ma: Known as "the black mother" and has a dual personality, exhibiting traits of gentleness and love, revenge and terrible death. *Known as "Wife of Shiva."* In the Holy Trinity she is Prakriti (Nature). She has black skin, a hideous face smeared with blood, fur arms. She despises most males and is ruler of regeneration, revenge, fear, dark magic, sexual potency, protection of women.

Kami: The god of desire and ruler of physical love, pleasures, sensual desire, spring, women, flowers.

Karttikeya: The Chief war god who has *six heads* and *twelve arms*. Defender of the gods. Women cannot enter his temples. Ruler of Revenge, dark magic, war. *Krishna:* An Avatar of Vishnu (incarnation of him). His birth was announced by a star and angelic voices. Had 180 wives. It is said that Krishna *returns at the end of each age to save the righteous,* destroy sin, and establish goodness and holiness. (Does that sound familiar?) He is ruler of erotic delights, sexual pleasures, love, music, and savior from sins.

Kubera: A dwarf god of earth and treasures of the earth enthroned in the Himalayas. He is a fat, white, bejeweled, hideous dwarf with three legs and only eight teeth. Ruler of fertility, wealth, treasure, minerals, gold, silver, jewels, pearls, and precious stones.

Lakshmi: Goddess of love and beauty. She gave Indra the drink of *soma* (wise blood) from her own body so he could produce the illusion of birth-giving and become king of the devas. Ruler of good fortune, prosperity, success, love, and feminine beauty.

Manjusri: Patron of grammatical science and ruler of enlightenment, wisdom, civilization, books, and writing.

Mara: Master magician and ruler of illusion and dark magic.

Parvati: God of the Himalayas, the Virgin Mother goddess. She represents union of god and goddess, man and woman, and rules over desire and ecstasy.

Puchan: Leads souls to the afterworld, ruler of marriage, journeys, roads, cattle, meetings, prosperity, and material gain.

Rama: Princely incarnation of Vishnu. Hero god.

Rati: Goddess of sexual passions and wife of Rama. She rules over lust and sexual activities. ***The Ribhus:*** Elves who are the sons of Indra by Saranyu and are craft making gods who rule over herbs, crops, streams, creativity, and blessings.

Rudra: The lord of beasts, ancient Vedic god of the dead and prince of demons who rules healing, herbs, death, disease, the jungle, wild animals, the woodlands, intelligence, song, sacrifice, creation, wind, and judgment.

Sarasvati: The inventor and discoverer of Sanskrit of *soma* in the Himalayas. Graceful woman with white skin, wears a crescent Moon on her brow and is seated on a lotus flower. Ruler of the arts, science, music, poetry, learning, and teaching.

Savitri: The rising and descending aspects of the Sun. Has golden hair and is a goddess who rides in a car drawn by two horses. Given rule of rest, healing, long life, night, immortality, and dispels tribulation.

Shiva: Member of the Hindu *triad* with Brahma and Vishnu. The merciful fertility god also always represents great power and rules physical love, destruction, long life, healing, magic, strength, medicine, storms, warriors, weapons, cattle, rivers, fire, death, dance, rhythm, meditation, righteousness, and of course; judgment.

Siva Jnana-Dakshinamurti: The god of all wisdom ... one of dozens. Hence ruler of wisdom and meditation.

Siva Lingodbhava: The god of reproduction. Ruler of fertility and procreation.

Surya: The chief sun god, legend says he is the original source of *soma* which was given to the moon for distribution to other gods. Described as a dark red man with three eyes and four arms who rides a chariot pulled by seven mares, one for each day of the week. His powers include ruling measurement, waters, winds, domination, blessings, understanding, and spiritual enlightenment.

Tara: Rules over threats, knowledge, compassion, control, and enlightenment. She is the mother goddess who helped to control human sexuality in order to achieve spiritual enlightenment.

Tvashtar: He created magical weapons for the gods and rules over art, crafts, skill with the hands, creativity, source of all blessings, and granter of prosperity. The creator of *all things* and craftsman of the gods.

Uma: is the corn goddess who is part of the trinity of the great goddess. She rules beauty, fertility, harvest, crops, dark seasons, and yoga asceticism. Also, she mediates conflicts between Brahma and the other gods.

Vajrapani: The god of lightning. Similar to Pan and supposed ruler of woodlands, physical love, and ecstasy.

Varuna: The god of the sun (another endless duplication of a *sun* god). Judge of man's deeds. *Supposedly Created the heavens,* earth, and the air between them and also rules wind, law, magic, snakes, rivers, heavenly gifts, demons, oceans, the creative will, seasons, rain, the sun, truth, justice, punishment, death, rewards, and prophecy.

Vishnu: With three steps he measured the seven worlds. He is the intermediary between the gods and man. Sun god (another). Vishnu appears on Earth as a human avatar. Nine avatars are said to have already come, with a tenth yet to appear. He rules peace, success, power, love, strength, compassion, abundance, and victory.

Visvakarma: A god of craftsmen and creation. *The Creator and maintainer of everything in the universe,* (this begins to reveal the duplicity of all these deities over and over) he makes things hold their individual shapes. He is the ruler of animals, horses, building, smiths, creativity, weapon-making, architecture, and craftsmen.

Yama: Judgment god of the dead. (once again terrible duplication of rulership) the god of death, truth, righteousness, judges man's dharma (their duty), destiny, death, and punishment.

The parade of myths here is evidence of serious bewilderment, and covered with frequent duplication for almost every aspect of human life. The frailty of human existence when we do not comprehend something calls out for imagination, or legend, anecdotes, and fables if truth is not honored. So you can imagine the extent of misunderstanding in the midst of all our societies if a lineage and history is not carefully studied. You can, however, find that necessity of lineage and historical precision in the Bible!

Just to scratch the surface of the endless amount of beliefs by other besieged cultures, I am also including some small lists of deities still worshiped within some of the largest populations or past communities of our world today.

Chinese Gods—The Current Top Ten:

1) Monkey
2) Guan-Yu
3) Jade-Emperor
4) Eight-Immortals

Fairy Tales Forever?

5) Guan-Yin
6) Yen-Lo-Wang
7) Feng-Du
8) Ao-Chin
9) Dragon-Kings
10) Dao

Mayan Gods—The Current Top Ten:

1) Chac
2) Ah-Puch
3) Alphabet gods
4) Ixxhel
5) Itzamna
6) Kinich-Ahau
7) Acat
8) Backlum-Chaam
9) Hun-Hunahpu
10) Kukulcan

Norse Gods—The Current Top Ten:

1) Loki
2) Odin
3) Frigg
4) Thor
5) Freya

6) Baldur
7) Valkyries
8) Hel
9) Andvari
10) Fenrir

Egyptian Gods—The Current Top Ten:

1) Ra
2) Min
3) Isis
4) Amun-Ra
5) Thoth
6) Anubis
7) Osiris
8) Set
9) Bast
10) Horus

A list this long is virtually short, and a total list of all legendary figures in history would provide a perfect indication that the multi-god concept is not a real, possible truth. Can you begin to guess how many remain unlisted?

There is far too much conjecture about gods today to include all of them! Flooding the earth this very day are many idols and ideologies that will end up being the myths of tomorrow. The pathway towards the delusion of polytheism is very wide.

There is no stopping the directory of present-day myths and names that pose as some form of god. Each person who lives on earth is given their entire life to get to know their creator. However, a created being has free will and needs to actively *seek* the truth, or they will surely perish in the midst of fiction.

Along with the whole host of gods not mentioned here, another perceived deity to consider if a person wants to embrace polytheism today, would have be a very dangerous and controversial single person. His name is Sun Myung Moon (a self-proclaimed messiah); he and his Unification Church have influenced the press and countless millions of people. Is he god or are any of these legends really the one that you need to know in person? Another single person to claim the specific right to be called God was David Koresh, formerly associated with the Seventh-day Adventists. Koresh broke off, claimed he was the Christ himself, and armed his militia with hoarded illegal weapons that eventually lead the clan to destruction. His depravity even extended out to having sexual relations with minors in the name of his godhood and as part of their grooming.

In conclusion about polytheism versus actual truth: before anyone can convincingly and intricately introduce you to the one truth, you need to know what deceit has already been inflicted upon the innocent. I hope I have initiated just the smallest sample of what *truth* would have to look like if truth could amalgamate all of these legends into one conglomerate of some polytheistic multi-phased deity. It simply is not logical, practical, possible, or truthful. I think it might help to reflect on the past and some of the present bemusement so we can achieve closure.

What I urge you to examine is the Bible, what many people justly understand to be the Word of God. Here you will find the second commandment of the one true God, which is often misunderstood, and yet it is a resolute reflection of the first commandment. We are commanded not to have "any false gods" before the one true God, but also, we are not to make *any* graven image [or create an idol by our own thought]. On the one hand you can accept a mega-name set of gods, or believe upon the one true God who wants faithful individual allegiance. This demand of the almighty is not based on the construction of actual stone, gold, or bronze figures but rather it is about the *heart* of mankind. When people exclaim, "To *me,* god is —!" they have unashamedly created that graven image by inserting the parameters which suit their own likeness or support their own coveted values. We have no business creating God in our image; it results in idolatry.

There is only one God. He has loved us and sought us from the beginning of time. There is no spiritually ambiguous "god-object" who has good days or bad days. There surely is no set of gods set forth to rule specific aspects of the universe. Isn't one enough for you to honor, befriend, and believe? His love for us is immeasurable. The truth of this matter reveals the "one" gracious and merciful almighty God.

There cannot be a god or gods based on the cornucopia of guesswork or humankind's vast imagination. Instead, there is the one God biblically revealed, who is holy, loving, ever-giving, ever-vigilant to embrace sinners and bestow grace, and, most of all, He is the ever-redemptive single truth in *Christ*. Every other god turns out to be a manifestation of our own inspiration and those gods are made pliable to become something based on our proceedings. The one true God is not like shifting shadows based on our actions, but provides us truth regularly and loves us because that is who He is! You can find this verification in book of James in verse 1:17–18.

We are sinful, fallen creatures with an absolute need for forgiveness! None of these myths focuses on this fact. We need a redeemer. If you pray, read, discern, and seek biblical answers and finally come to that conclusion, then, in a broken and humble state, you will be drawn to the overwhelming decision to embrace the historically proven and inerrant documented life of Jesus. A lasting union is possible through His sacrifice of grace alone. He is exactly who he said he is—"the way, the truth, and the life"—and only God himself could say that and only God could make an eternal sacrifice for sin through His death on a cross. He *is* God incarnate and he did say, "The Father and I are One," (John 10:30) and thus the only worthy sacrifice for sin. May your decision to receive the truth, give you a peace that will forever secure your eternal life and give you strength to reject the spiritual separation which has been induced by fables, myths, and fairy tales!

What will *you* choose to embrace onward into eternity: fairytales, or faith?

Chapter 4

One More Try!

If at first you don't succeed, try, try, again. Have you ever wondered why there are only two *try* words in that idiom? Why aren't there three, four, ten, or many more? If the ultimate goal is important and you have assurance that it "can" be done, why would you stop at just a few attempts? No individual would quit trying if they categorically believed that it could be done and that any action or mission could certainly reach the desired goal. In most cases, though, people do give up when the ordeal seems so daunting that it appears to have no chance. The biggest step then is for the person to engage another ingredient, step out in faith, and give one more try.

The Bible has a myriad of scriptures that show people of faith. In the book of Ruth, we can find that in a time when honor lacked for outsiders and women of no offspring loomed darkly, hope could only ring true with continued pursuit of true faith. She endures and receives help. She is blessed and redeemed and sees a change from poverty to wealth and from a barren widow to being married and becoming a mother. All this was changed through faith and trying.

Separated by nine hundred miles, Ezekiel and Jeremiah both gave the message of repentance and chastised the defiant Jews. The faith of these men to stand against the common form of error in the shape of rebellion was powerful. These prophets were also identical in their voice of "turn around" and "repent" or face the consequence. For those listeners that found themselves following the men of faith there would be refreshing and a tone of redemption to come. But in that time listening to a message that proclaimed righteousness was a battle for most and it would require a deep routed faith to endure.

More sound biblical evidence will show that Ezra finds that faith is derived by seeing even pagan kings moved by the almighty to serve the will of God. He shows what miracles truly are and it comes from the power of God, not just coincidence. He sees that purity of life makes the miracle of God's hand even clearer and more distinct. His faithful and righteous handling of gold and also the people of exile, earns him the favor of the Lord. That faith comes from a lineage of descendants that is almost two pages long, and he gets to see the Israelites whom had been exiled, return to the Jerusalem.

The book of Hebrews in the New Testament, written by a Jew himself, is seen by most biblical scholars to contain an unmatched list of the faithful and those who had miraculous intervention in their lives. The list of names that Paul uses to promote dutiful living and trust in God is profound. In the book of Hebrews, chapter eleven, you will find a list that is historically accurate and masterfully chosen names of the beloved to show the Jews that trust is the key to redemption and moving in faith results in the miracle of God's power. The faithfully devoted like Abraham, Isaac, Jacob, Joseph, Jochebed and Amram, the parents of Moses, and of course Moses himself, Joshua, Rahab, Gideon, Samson, Barak, Jephthah, David, Samuel, and countless others all whom stayed faithful and took that extra step. These are all indications of what we have to do if we are interested in trying again. We have it in us! After all it is Jesus, a Jew, and "the Christ," that confirms that we are all human with a spiritual nature from the creator and that God is at hand in all women and men.

What I hope to reveal is that although we are all three part beings; spirit, soul, and body, and even though the reminiscence of God may exist in all his created, the truth and saving quality will never become evident without a try again a miracle. That is because we are also all saturated with the fall of humanity and we are all sinners. (see Romans 3:23).

Consequently, we have all disobeyed God at some point and that makes us sinners. "If we say that we have no sin, we deceive ourselves, and the truth is not in us. If we confess our sins, he is faithful and just to forgive us [our sins], and to cleanse us from all unrighteousness. If we say that we have not sinned, we make him a liar, and his word is not in us" (1 John 1:8—1:10). This is quite a scary thought. If we believe we have not sinned, we are deceived and we *make God a Liar*. I would not call God a liar, would you? If you have not reached the conclusion that all of us are flawed and have disobeyed God at some point, then you should try again. We need to keep trying to discover the plan of deliverance or we assert that we are without any need of saving.

The miracle is that God interceded and took the punishment and served a *just* sentence of death for all the sin of every person and eradicated our errors and we were made clean by His holy hand. The most common misapprehension by people is that God is a good God and will simply forgive us. Just forgiving or ignoring sin is not just. A truly good God is actually just. For instance; if you sat in a trial where you had suffered a horrid event in which the perpetrator had just stolen all your goods from your home, killed you children, raped your wife and burned your home. If you then heard the judge state to the criminal, "you seem nice, you seem sad, you seem sorry ... you are forgiven, you may go!" Would you ever, in your wildest dreams, conclude, "Oh, that judge is *good*"? No, you would never think anything like that, because "good" is not an inconsistency; rather, goodness is *just*. To clear the sins of the human race by just winking at sin is not good. Something needs to be done to accomplish justice. That is a supernatural intervention when the creator steps in where no individual could accomplish the truth. The good news (Gospel) of what God has done for us, is something that he will complete supernaturally, but only if we believe the need and surrender to the fact that we cannot clean ourselves. So my point is that sharing the Gospel news with stern perseverance is the only real act of *faith* in the matters of the heart.

Why keep trying?

"Greg, are you really going to put yourself through that again?" remarked Debbie woefully.

"You spent years working on that thing the first time, hijacked my dinning room table from the birth of Tarah until she was 14, and for what?"

"All that happened is many of your friends no longer want to talk to you, you were up for hours every night, and all you do is cry when you think about them not getting the message."

"You know, it is possible they just don't want to hear it."

Those were the words from my beloved wife when I said I had been considering writing another book. I had been working on four chapters and getting nowhere. I told her I hoped I could get the message out clearer this time. I also explained why I would just keep trying and trying even though the simple message of "get saved or perish" was falling on deaf ears. I know it is a calling and commandment for every believer, and certainly me. It is a mission from God for certain; if we do not get saved we will die in our sins.

Greatly fatigued, I expounded, "That is possible you know, but there have been dozens of great remarks about my first book and many lives changed also, because of the good news."

"I just want my dearest friends to hear what so many strangers have heard, and been moved!"

I surely do know the biblical explanation of why the message is not received, that can be viewed in (Luke 8:1-15) and also (Mathew 13:1–23) and refereed to by Mark as he revealed the idea of the seed as the word of God. I understand the parable of Christ and the Word (seeds) which is given to all, but sometimes landing in thorn bushes where it is choked, or gravel where it cannot grow, or to being eaten by birds (stolen by the world's viewpoint) or even when it falls on fertile places where a person claims to believe for a while and then eventually they balk at all Christian principles and Bible values.

I know why it is not received by people who think their final destiny and judgment is based on works (actions) and why they will always feel offended. They will naturally conclude that I am condemning them for an inferior lifestyle or comparing myself to them and claiming they have a greater degree of sinfulness.

Nothing could be further from the truth. Rather, I think resistance comes because no one wants to consider the truth is an *all or nothing* devotion to faith with God. But as long as I am alive, I will hope that the message from me can become fruitful. For I know that the Word itself is infallible, and if my presentation is the stumbling block, even God can fix that. Otherwise, my only conclusion is that those who hear the message despise me and that I myself am seen as an evil link to misunderstanding.

I have grievously experienced the pain of many friends who misconstrue words on purpose, ignore the message about *all* people being sinners, just to make me out to be the bad guy. I have had difficulty explaining that I myself am destine for hell, if not for the power of the cross and God's merciful Gospel because I too am sinful. If I were to surmise that I am the failing factor, I would also need to tell Debbie I am obviously not doing a good enough job. However, that is wrong because it is God's scriptural word which explains that the germination of seeds to receive faith in Christ alone is done by the Holy Spirit whereas we are only planters of the seed.

It is my flesh and personal battle with my own lack and simple human frailty that make me assume I have to push and push! My impatience is undoubtedly an element in my own perception of what is being ingested or ignored. Why do I force so much and cram so much into my discussions and attempts to convey love through the word of the Bible? That is a simple answer: I know the inexorable knowledge of a fatal end consequence without Jesus. An unremitting reason for persistence is my knowledge and experience. Sharing the truth is not just a passing fancy, but an actual miracle. I know that the harvest is plentiful if people want to know the Gospel, but the "workers are few" (Matt 9:36–38, Luke 10:2–3). This is why I push to an exasperating degree.

While I was once discussing the Gospel and the process of sharing with one of my friends, Tim, a believer himself, he paused and thought hard and I am certain the Holy Spirit gifted him with his explanation. He said, "You do it because you know the consequence of not believing and you want to get it all done at once. You feel if they do not get a full dose at that very moment you may never have a chance again." This was brilliant, and it should have relaxed me to rest in the peace of knowing God can do all things. I cannot force such a divine message of the Gospel, but only try again. I should never imagine that I am the sole source of the fruition of the Gospel. I should try again if I can, but serve through prayer if I might not receive another chance of sharing.

Trying involves effort, background, understanding, education, and motivation. I have all of the tools and surely the desire, thus it is an indisputable fact I will continue to seek out my loved ones and friends as well as strangers, with the Good News. The Bible is the Word of God and any real push to learn that certitude will reveal the abundance of legitimacy and of course the Holy Spirit will provide the faith to believe. The great news of eternal life is not only joyous, but moreover it is uncomplicated and certain.

If you desire to be free from the burden of sin and the eventual tragic aftermath. Then you can be saved! You must believe with your heart, mind, body and soul, and confess with your mouth that *Christ alone* is Lord and redeemer and then you unequivocally will be saved (Rom 10:9). No deeds, no actions, no myth, no requirement to perform "dead" acts of repentance, but instead turn away from sin by knowing it has been removed by the cross and the debt is paid. That is the Gospel of the Lord.

So, if you think you know all there is to know about eternity and you have not chosen the Gospel, then maybe you should just try, try again.

Chapter 5

Divine Mercy, a Reasonable Verdict!

There are hundreds, thousands, even millions of stories about survival or what people might call miracles. In just one individual's ordinary lifetime, escape from death or extraordinary supernatural intervention would be conceded as great fate. Many or multiple such exploits would not just be remarkable, but rather a testimony. To review one life and see many incidents of intersession, this indicates a pattern and signifies more than the possibility of just luck. I am so convinced of miraculous stories in my own life which suggest supernatural intervention I feel it is worth expression.

I use the word miracle to constitute a supernatural movement or caress of God's hand so that the result provides glory to provider. A miracle is not just a natural phenomenon, marvel, or portent. Rather it is veritably something that shows attentiveness, love, and exalts the provider because it could not be attained by just nature. So my definition of the word miracle is not the common one used in our world today, it is not just an extremely rare or coincidental passing of intense happenstances or an accumulation of human greatness. In every one of these situations either I, or a friend, or other people would have been in grave or fatal danger if the order of things had transpired differently without God.

The first such apparent miracle I can recall is when I was a very young toddler and I had sustained a one hundred and four-degree temperature for a number of hours, even stretching into the next day, to such an extent my teeth even became green-spotted. Doctors made house calls in those days, and the normal fever-reducing techniques were not working. It did not appear that they would, so the recommendation was to go to the hospital. My parents got through this with prayer and devotion, and the fever broke to the one hundred mark before they got another hospital doctor to examine again. Well, that seems to be a normal string of events, you might say. Minor as it may be, I think it was prayer resulting in a miracle. I know for certain that fifty-five years ago, a temperature of that intensity for such a long period was often in the arena of fatality.

If you find yourself thinking these stories seem all too ordinary, minor, or by simple chance, please just be patient and you will read some which challenge the senses and imagination. Some of the stories seem common but then end up revealing circumstances more substantial than just coincidence.

The next occasion I recall was another miracle for parents, considering what might have been. While I was climbing a neighbor's tree I plummeted head first over 20 feet, at the age of eight. My Mom grabbed a blanket and wrapped me and off we went to Mountainside Hospital. As we drove, she was speaking but the words were not distinguishable. She later told me how frantically concerned she was that I was not waking up or responsive, yet I was aware of every turn and every bump in the road, and I could clearly see her face. She explained to me that I never opened my eyes. I remember the ride, as clear as ever to this current day. After being examined, I had suffered no neck injury, back injury, or breaks, no real problem other than apparent unconsciousness. A fall of that nature can surely kill or maim, but I sustained no serious injury other than a concussion. It most likely was a miracle, compassionate supernatural intercession rather than just random. The Lord's ways are perplexing to say the least.

Surely, I think this next event was the most chilling in my life at the time it happened. It seems I was not a very obedient boy in some ways even though my parents were delightfully disciplined and Godly in nature. Sometimes I would not hesitate to fib just to get what I wanted. I would go out to play and say I was headed to Tuers Park but actually I was headed to the stream and the fields. We had great expeditions there and one of the best of many such adventures involved a concrete spillway with an opening about ten feet high that had a wrought iron rail preventing entrance. The surrounding contradiction there was that it had rusted and half of the rails had broken off to create the perfect place to grab, pull up to the top of the spillway, and settle on the bars. This made it easy to look inside the tunnel, and some other kids eventually pushed large limbs over the mouth so you could jump down in and climb back out.

We would bring boots, candles, flashlights, and matches. We could run up the concrete spillway over the bars, stop, and then down the limb into the eighth foot tall tunnel. That one formidable day started great and we walked close to half a mile in the tunnel under the Garden State Parkway drainage. As we approached the highway, inlets we came up to a huge gate dripping with water on all sides and trickling over the top. It was a creepy-looking thing, like a witch's castle entrance. The gate was actually a flood barrier with an apparatus at the top which could have triggered at any time. When we saw this, the realization of the inevitable was so frightening all I could do was shout, "Run, Don!" We moved at a frantic pace back to the entrance in record time splashing and trampling through rocks and other debris. Still in shock we got to the big limb climbed up and out and then decided to do the unforgivable to any other explorers, we knocked down the limb into the huge tunnel to foil any more of the inquisitive. Never was there such an explosive beating in my chest, burning on my sweaty brow, and lurching in my stomach. We had avoided potential drowning.

Now, you might not think that was a miracle, but as I left the scene, I had sworn an oath to God that I would never return. However, the temptation that very next day was far too great, and I had to go see. In only sneakers this time, I got to the fields and ran up the spillway. At the top, I did the usual pause to look over and beheld what was to be the most consuming fright imaginable. I could see the water only a foot from reaching over the spillway. I could hardly contain my breakfast almost puking into the dark engrossing water below. I was paralyzed with dismay pondering the possible horrid demise and grotesque end which we had narrowly escaped.

We were given mercy and a miracle that it had not opened with tons of water gushing into us, burying flashlights, candles, and boots all tumbling and rolling into a tight little exit tube at one end with which we were all too familiar. We would have been pinned by thousands of gallons of liquid runoff. The miracle was that the barrier trigger had somehow delayed long enough to spare our lives, even with our loud splashing and clattering to get away. No new rain or water that came, just a little time, obviously opening some time in the night after our visit.

I do not recall the turn of events that lead me to decide that another form of tunnel exploration was once again safe, but later that year, in winter, we went to foolishly investigate the one under Grove Street. It would be safer, and of course we knew that tunnel very well. It was eight feet at the one end and nobody could get to it unless you tried to swim into it or swung in off the tree that hung over the right side of the tunnel area. To get back out of the tunnel just a six foot run and jump across the water and grab the vines on the tree. Piece of cake, eh? Well I guess my foolishness and previously blessed recovery had not made me any more sensible. It was winter, many months after our horrid scare, and boots were an expected ensemble when leaving the house. So, once again I went off claiming to be going to the park to play (a bald faced lie) and I was headed for adventure.

I had been through this tunnel before; it was wide, with no tight spots. It was snowy and there was some ice, but we still had the vine for a boost. We went with the usual ease across the opening and headed underneath the road. We trudged through the water and got to the other side under the street but found getting out of this side in winter was not going to be easy on the other side because the greenery was dead. So we decided to return back through the tunnel. When we got to the side where we had entered we were poised to jump and head back home. Don was first with a zip and done, but when it came to my turn, there was no such ease of operation.

I stepped to the edge of the slab and the moss which was there even in the frosty conditions and it was far too slippery to make a good spring board, so I went sliding but good. I slammed down on the ice, yet it did not break right away. I tried to move like a good boy scout, lying flat and wide while sliding to spread the weight. It was working I thought and Don kept encouraging me, "Spread out and move slowly, Greg." I was getting close to the embankment and the icy cold wet must have made me stupid and too anxious. I started to stand and immediately when through the ice like a bullet. The water was like nothing I had ever experienced; it was pins and needles, and only seconds had passed before it was debilitating.

Worth Another Try

The pool of water under the ice slabs was surely ten feet deep or more, from our recollection in the summer months. So standing on the bottom was not an option. My boots were filling with water and far too heavy to swim. I actually was certain I was going to be pulled under the ice just a couple feet behind me. My hands were too cold and wet, and my head and face were soaked too, so the incredibly short struggle almost appeared to be at an end. I whimpered, "I can't!" Don raced to a tree and ripped off a sizable dead branch. He tossed it over the ice, and it slapped the surface and broke only one part of the ice. My hands slipped every time I tried to grab it, so I knew he would not be able to pull me out. I was completely numb now. It was over! I was convinced it was over.

At the moment when all natural possibilities were exhausted I heard inside me a voice urging me, "back, back!" But going backwards in this pool of frozen water was beyond any sense whatsoever because the ice would surely cover me and keep me down. Then when I said, "Hold on!" and sloshed backwards Don later told me he thought I was giving up and was committing myself to the deep. Instead, in those 10 feet of water my soggy, sopping boots hit something that felt solid. Sure enough, it was a huge boulder. I pushed and had gained some stability above the water. Don got another branch and fortunately the rest is history.

I had been saved by the rock! What a wonderful miracle. When I think back though (with sarcasm here) I am positive it could not have been divine intervention, rather I guess the internal voice instructing me was just a duck that swam by and said, "Quack, quack," and I thought, "Back, back!" What do you think?

Not good enough Eh! Ok, so hold on they get better. I do not want these to get boring so I will try to make them quick, because God has been so merciful to me it is not just enlightening but remarkable, so I do not want to ruin the joy.

Next story; I was eleven just turning twelve and had been given the delight of every man's fancy. I was invited to go on a Boy Scout trip even though I was not legal "scout age" yet. "O my goodness," I assured myself, I will no doubt behave on this trip, because it was a gift from my brother and the Scout Master. Plans were made, it would be an unforgettable trip, it was under way. This would probably end up to be the one of the most instructive trips ever.

Here I was hiking out to Scout Lake with troop five and I chose to run out in front of everyone to show my prowess. I sighted something just to the side of the path and it appeared to be under a rock but still visible. Yep, it was something: a book. I grabbed at it and pulled it out and sure enough it was a Bible. Upon reaching me the Scout Master accepted it and he decided to bless the boys with a little Word. He cracked it open, and the priceless expression on his face was one that might never be matched. Inside someone had carved out the center of the pages and placed a few ounces of weed. This turned into one of the most demonstrative examples of proper behavior that I ever witnessed. The leaders went through hours of extremely

Worth Another Try

taxing work turning it over to the Police. Most folks would have probably used it or tossed it in the garbage. I felt I had made the trip a real wing ding, what excitement!

So, to celebrate I got up the next morn before anybody and went to the lake to explore. "Cool look over there," I thought, "it's a little bit of rope." I grabbed it and slipped around a branch and was ready for fun to the max with my imagination. I looked out on the lake saw the dam at one end and it was wide enough to walk, most likely it was eighteen or twenty inches wide. What a day this would be. I scurried back and forth for quite some time creating ripples with my imaginary boat. I got to the end turned around one last time and tried to move faster. Smart move buddy! Brilliant, except for the unseen shoe lace which was unraveling with each move I made.

It was only a second or two but it seemed an eternity and of course it went in slow motion. I saw it coming, thought about it happening, and then stepped right on it. Smack went my foot directly into my other foot and tangled with shoe lace, rope, and my branch toy boat. I dangled for a second and my twisted motion was sending me down the side of the forty foot drop with jagged rocks at the bottom. When sure enough, out of nowhere, a *huge* whale jumped out of the lake!

No, what really happened was my unyielding contortion towards the death drop actually spun me, almost as if I was *pushed* and it plunged me into the water on the other side of the dam. It was a blessing that my impossible tilt was corrected by falling in the opposite direction and into the lake rather than certain death. I know the finest gymnast in the world could not have pulled that off to save the day. So! At that very moment, at that very moment was once again another miracle!

Now, don't get tired of hearing that, because there are lots more to come. All of these calamities up till now some folks might choose to dismiss as pure luck or coincidence, but other circumstances in my life were absolute saves; there is no doubt in my mind.

Shortly after getting my driver's license I was very fortunate to get a rusted, shore kept, non-running, Volkswagen Beetle the summer before my eighteenth birthday. In fact, I became the talk of the town after a new distributor, wheels, running boards, door panels, floor panel, master cylinder, brake lines, and a paint job where the boys from Earl Scheib exclaimed, "First I gotta see if paint'll stick tah this thing." What an amazing chore it was to get it finished. My father was even so loving and proud he would take it Sundays after church and display it in the front row of the golf club. There you could view vehicles owned by the membership early comers to the course, a row of the finest autos in the nation. There was a presentation of Lamborghini, Maserati, Ferrari, Cadillac, Volvo, Mercedes, a yellow '65 VW Beetle, and a Porsche. What an impressive collection.

That vehicle was so much fun; still it lost a wheel once. By the way, when they tell you never to use a *ten-penny* nail rather than a cotter pin because it will rust, let's just say it is a fairly gut wrenching feeling watching your own wheel pass by you on the road, as you scurry into oncoming traffic! The Bug also was up on two wheels in a traffic circle because of a pickup that cut me off. Hence, "Harry" earned a printed tape label on the glove box which exclaimed, "Beware and welcome!" "But please ride at your own risk, Harry has a few imperfections."

The most defining issue Harry had was not even age or rust, or even some of the rattles. You see, the problem with Beetles is they have independent suspension and no springs, just basically shocks. Independent of the rest of the car is what it was. When it would go up on a lift the wheels would tilt inwards and cock under like a *bug*. And this was how my miracle came to pass. Near Greenwood Lake, New Jersey, there is a very winding road called Old Black Hill Road if memory serves. There is one curve that presents trouble for many. In fact, the tow truck driver arrived to the site, and when I asked why this was so dangerous and why no one had made a change, his reply was, "They put up a sign: Slow to 15 mph."

The car was traveling about 25 or 30 miles per hour but I guess the sign which said slow to 15 mph was not positioned quite right. Harry lifted the two left wheels and then they landed them in the tucked position. The neighbor down the road exclaimed, "We could hear you comin' for about 15 seconds." The car flipped and dragged for sixty feet before it flipped again. My arm went out the window and dragged along the pavement for just a flash and then my shoulder also. Neither ended up scarred, and my limbs were not ripped off, but the crash of the roof and the glass in my lap was very frightening.

When it stopped, I sprang out of it like a James Bond movie, certain it was going to explode.

There was such an impact from the car flip it crushed the roof to down to my belly, rather than eye level where it normally stood. The left rear wheel had cracked in two, like the breaking of an early morning doughnut. The roof was almost touching the steering wheel and the door collapse like a V, but the miracle here had actually been in pre-plan, if you can imagine. Earlier I had been working on the floor boards under the driver side with pop rivets and sheet metal which is what much of the car body had intertwined, but I had left it unfinished because I felt I would have a better idea on the structure to strengthen it later. I never figured to get pushed through the floor. The crushing of the roof and pushing of the seat through the floor saved my neck and back and who knows what else. Once again fate had dealt me another perfect hand. Or was it Holy intercession?

Remember, I mentioned I was just getting started with the tales. I am ashamed to say that as a young college man, I was still not functioning in the mode of operation that would be pleasing to my Lord. Although I was insistent to my friends that I had no interest, they wanted a roaring bachelor party for me. I asked that there not be any of the typical lechery. But boys will be boys, and most of them wanted to get the festivities to a high pace. I joined in to placate my good buddies. But this wore me down and disturbed me because I knew I was going to be wed soon and I knew I wanted to be more suitable to a family man and walk a proper Christian walk, even though my actions up to then were mostly quite contrary.

The longer the party went on the worse the abuse of the body. I was drinking and making merry with mind-altering paraphernalia. I was getting so angry at my ugly condition that in a short time, I was placing myself under extreme condemnation. The weariness of sin had lead me to a problem because I was sick of my own lack of control. Without making a big deal of this, let's just say I wanted to make it go away. I was under no condition to be at a party having fun, and now I was thinking irrationally.

I was so woozy, depressed, and upset I was prepared to do what so many precious young people consider when faced with their own horrid actions. I was thinking of taking my own life. I was so in love with the Lord but wanted to show all my pals that a "Jesus freak" was normal also, but this caused me to be just like any sinner without the perspective of purpose. So, I walked away from the party and my idea was to taunt the cars on the boulevard. I was on the curb, and they were moving at a good clip. I did it a few times, and the last car even honked as he passed and it seemed mighty close. I was determined to make someone else kill me because I was distressed but acting like a coward. It came down to the last chance. I stepped off the curb, and the car was cruising directly at me, but instead of the horrifying crunch and thud I was expecting, I was thrown to the curb. Under no means was it by my own thrust or the car that sped past.

Of course, one might not want to believe it was a throw or push; it was not a stumble, not a trip, not even a lunge at the last second. Rather, I was hurled to the curb as if a comic strip hero ran at me and knocked me over to the sidewalk. I explained later that it felt like an enormous hand willfully escorting me out of the way with passion. The tingles of a touch from God or a push from an angel can be a beautiful thing but it can also be chilling. The figurative portent or aberration really seemed gracious but angry at my foolishness. There is no more sickening feeling than knowing that the love of God never gives up on you no matter how often or sadly you fail. Pulled out of another lethal transgression I was again given a break. That night, *someone threw me supernaturally* out of danger. I believe there is no reason for any spirit to care about me except for the one who made me. I know it was a miracle but these things are not substantive to people so most choose to doubt the veracity.

Are you tired of hearing about one man's life and the incredible number of events which demonstrate a care outside the natural world? Well this next one actually involved another person performing an intervention to save my bacon. I was no longer a newlywed, and we had youngsters and were invited to the New Jersey shore to stay with my brother in a rather extravagant and expansive house. The week was delightful. By the last day or two, I wanted to get up and out at the crack of dawn and explore the ocean and do some body surfing without the family. So I headed to the beach, and I played in the ocean and hit the waves feverishly. It was well over two hours out there

Worth Another Try

and now closer to three. I had done my bid for the Olympic body surfing championships, but I am actually not good, and thus I began a much more fun game. I was doing the baseball catcher stance and catching waves as they ferociously tumbled me over and over. I got one last enormous blast and it kept me under and splashed me in a twirl for a sustained length of time and quite a lot of skidding in the sand. I popped up from the surf and was thrilled at the big boom but was dizzy and filled with sand everywhere.

I jumped back in and swam out where I could float and slosh water into my suit and just completely engage the water for some deep cleansing. I was swimming out just past the sand bar and figured I was ready to go in now. When I tired, it came upon me, I realized here I am again in the middle of something that does not even seem like part of my life. I was over my head, swimming, and going nowhere. I dropped down to touch the sand bar and it was not there. I did not panic but after several attempts to surf in or swim in I was not touching the bottom or moving inward. OK, so I know as a boy scout that the proper method of survival in an undertow is to not swim on top but instead swim sideways till you can make a turn and go into the shoreline. These numerous attempts were not working for the life of me, so to speak. I was still not going to panic but knew I was going to be without strength very soon, minutes if not seconds. It was still so early in the day there was not a soul on the beach, in sight or within screaming distance. This was so infuriating, I was not able to advance and if I went under I found the sand about one foot below standing level, but insufficient to use for pushing. You hear about these things but they never happen to you or anyone you know. Now was time for panic! I was going to be pulled under by a rip tide or undertow.

Two minutes turned to five and five turned to seven and it was obvious I did not even have the strength to yelp or even form a screechy whistle which was the loudest thing I could do. Every attempt to produce a loud sound was pitifully swallowed by the waves around me and my every breath was needed to make a decision. Now I was panicked! I even had the strangest thought which I whispered aloud. I said, "What the hell am I going to say to my parents to explain this when I am dead." No doubt I was in trouble, but just like that, right on queue, I see the crew coming down the street and onto the beach. It was my family, my Dad, Mom, brother and his kids and my daughters and wife Debbie.

I still could not get the words our or even squeak to signal them. So when they got there my brother was first in the water and first to be near enough for communication. I squawked and squealed and asked for help, begging him towards me. Mike is 6 foot 7 seven inches tall, and he truly thought I was playing a game or acting out a part. He was walking only ten feet away from me and wasn't struggling a bit. I was going down for the third time and my brother was thinking it was practical joke. He somehow was able to stand on the sand bar reach out and our fingers touched and then grabbed. My feet kicked and I peddled like a doggy paddle and in a few seconds they were touching sand and my head was jut above the surface. God provided the perfect timing again.

I have not set foot in the ocean with water over my chest since that very day over two decades ago. This was not just a close call, it was a miracle, and I do not believe anyone knew how close it was.

Had enough? Are you beginning to see that every single life (including mine) has far more mercy than anyone deserves? It's a God thing ... just face it! If not convinced, then here we go!

I was a furniture mover for six years and I had some very close calls. The circumstance surrounding each of them actually seemed normal within a life of moving heavy objects all day, which is naturally going to be dangerous. There was a time when we were traveling back from Smoke Rise, New Jersey a fairly exclusive area for homes. On the highway before we got to Wayne, New Jersey we encountered a very miraculous traffic accident. It was not so much for us as it was for the other group nearby. The rain was coming down cats and dogs like never before. We were traveling eastbound on Interstate 80 and I saw a strange glistening ahead in the deluge.

I remarked to Ray the driver, "something's up ahead." he was quiet and didn't respond, I said again, "did you see that?" To me it looked like a police light because it went round and round in a flashing circle but no blue just red and white. In a moment and in the downpour we could not see anything until it was far too late.

Turns out, the spinning lights were the headlights, sidelights, and taillights of a big passenger bus, skidding in the water on the highway. By the time we were upon it nothing could be done. Ray shouted, "It's a freakin'... bus!" He did not use the word *freaking*, but that was unimportant, then and now. All he tried would not stop or move the wheels of the truck. It was inevitable that we were going to hit the bus broadside. The miracle I got to see in the midst of the flash and slamming, banging, and crashing was this! We hit the bus which had spun out of control attempting to exit and then coming back onto the highway, blocking two of three lanes. Phenomenally, we hit it at exactly the right time so the impact threw it out of the way of the five or six cars directly behind us. There was not as much as the hiss of swerving or screech or honking or crunch, just swooshing, nobody was prepared.

We collided and straightened out a vehicle which was across two and a half lanes of interstate traffic in a three lane spot. Our injuries would turn out not to be critical. The crash was substantial and loud, but did it not stop me from hearing and fully realizing the instantaneous particulars right after our impact. Two cars on the scene simply swished by us on the right side and then three more in between the bus and the truck, it happened so acutely it was like it was a cartoon. We had knocked the bus out of collision range and that avoided a pileup for these cars which were directly to the rear and next to us during this pathetic downpour.

Had we been seconds later and the cars been first on the scene they would have plunged into the luggage compartments on the sides and also hit the engine in the rear of this bus. It would have been a nasty pile up. In this instance; I was not the receiver experiencing the blessing, rather it was five cars directly in line for a devastating dilemma. Here I was just a witness to another anomalous episode.

The ensuing talk with the boss on the phone has to be added in this chapter for comic relief and to divulge the kind of boss we had in this job at the time. The truck was towed to a Gas station and Ray and I went in to use the phone and the explanation from Ray went like this. "Bill, Hey Bill, Greg and I were in an accident." This was followed by a pause of just a few seconds on our end as I listened in. Next came Ray's response to Bill's first obvious retort, "Yep, *it's* alright!" Ray covered the phone mouthpiece and we laughed. Amazing question eh, the truck, the truck, yeah ... the truck! Concern for the employee was never top of the list with Bill.

I know that the Lord was looking after the people around us that night and our big truck had most likely saved lives by pushing the bus out of the road. Clearly the event protected them from a crash that would have been brutal.

Another such narrow escape for me was during one of many commercial moves. We used to take even dangerous jobs which qualified riggers would turn down, thanks to Bill's relentless desire for profit. These were jobs where they required stair-climbers. Other proper equipment was substituted with our brawn. We could not use the elevator because of the size and weight of this one considerable safe. So it got attached to a fairly exclusive hand truck which had the rollers on the sides to smooth our way down stairs. This hand truck was made for heavy dressers or a refrigerator, not this kind of lifting. So we did a lot of binding with ties and straps and headed to the stairs.

The guiding down the stairs went fairly well until we got to the next to last landing. At that moment the two men at the top had the straps break and rip off. The load went the last few steps at a pace that was uncontrolled, bang, bang, bang, and a huge thump. It got to the turn and stood straight up with me in the corner. Ray moved aside best he could, but the thing trapped my knee and squashed it. I ended up sandwiched on the inner side, and our strong man Ray was on the outside. My head was in that very position seconds before the crunch between wall and safe, and it would have sounded much like a melon popping when stomped or dropped from a window. My last thought when I heard the strap and felt the immense weight was, "Lord God, please save me." My knee got pinned as it stood straight up, and squashed ... no room for a *head* there. Close call absolutely, so I guess it was just my prowess *alone* as an acrobat and my balance escape technique that was the saving factor ... nope! *Not a chance!* I think we all know what it was!

Now for the *pièce de résistance*. This time the incident was when I was in line to become a supervisor and the current driver was on his way out. Much like these other circumstances and stories, I would love to heighten the intensity and make all the references to the exact place and time. However, I have tried to block this one from my mind because of the distasteful agony I would go through each time I thought of the horror, ugliness, and ensuing life-altering result had there been no miracle. I do remember the facts.

The driver had positioned the truck in the loading bay for a commercial move with a setup for dozens of fireproof filing cabinets and many heavy desks. This kind of move was going to require precise dolly expertise and movement. He had been drinking and actually not recovered from the night before, so it was not a hangover but instead he was a mess and drunk. He had not put the truck in the right position and thus it made the ramps to the tailgate cocked to the side (angled). I had to set this up properly so I could start the work while he was doing paperwork and insurance. The ramps just weren't right.

I bent down and tugged at it but no way would they square up from the dock, they were stuck in place. Still, I tried again and the one on the left moved a little and it was able to be placed almost straight. The ramp on the right was not going to be moved and Jim had taken the keys and gone off to chatter with the customer. I jumped down into the bay and walked over to the left ramp which I had almost corrected at first and now was able to get it right. The right ramp was much tougher though so I pushed and pushed and it pop up from the snagged position. I settled it in the proper square position, but not to any degree of perfection, and I was determined to make just one more adjustment.

Then without warning I heard a voice as if it were a person next to me. The voice said, "Move, Greg!" Now most ideas, inclinations, or even instincts do not include a salutation and name directly to the psyche. But when the Holy Spirit speaks to a believer it is so nurturing, assertive, and legitimate, so I instantly moved sideways away from the tailgate, which was at my heart level. In only a fraction of a second the huge truck shook, bounced, shuddered, and rolled into the bay fully sending the ramps into the aluminum garage door reducing it to a mass of twisted metal. It gained enough momentum in that short 6-foot lunge that it even bounced a few times against the rubber stoppers at the dock.

I became flush, grabbed my head, and I cannot count the number of times I cried, "Oh my God, oh my God, oh my God!" The resulting scene would have been ghastly for the paramedics to witness. Had I not been instructed to move, the path of the tailgate would have had no option but to slice me in half. Not precisely in half, but I feel the phrase still applies. I had more emotions at that time than ever before in my life. Jim had left the truck slightly in gear but had not set the parking brake. This kind of mistake was one of his last, but for me this miracle was another gift of love from above. My life had been spared in glorious reality, once again.

A miracle is supernatural intercession. I have pointed out that the errant common use has lessened the glory that was once a part of knowing God cares and is alive and watching all things. I know that the Lord spoke to me that day and rescued me many other days because the eventual plan was a glorious wife and two extraordinary daughters. This plan was not going to be thwarted and silenced by a drunken error of someone who was horribly careless. I think many people with as much determination as I have would have kept working to set the ramps right and would face this nightmare problem, but I was *commanded to move,* and I did. Some individuals would not want to be commanded to do anything, and that is why Christ offers salvation freely. Still, I see the love of my Holy Father in heaven as the most glorious thing I own, since He has given me the Word of truth to know and also provided salvation to keep me by his side eternally. I will continue to be in awe over the grace and mercy which he gives, which bears testimony to that which he offers anyone.

    I have survived many more events in my life that could be construed as miraculous. I was pushed from a balcony over ten feet head first. I was hit by the branches of a falling two-ton tree trunk. As a youth, I was stuck yet once again in a tunnel for an inordinate time, pinned side to side and somehow with my pleading and seeking mercy, I was freed. I jumped from a two story house and landed in building debris, my foot still has the scar from the nail. I swam back in the canal to that friend's house in one of the New Jersey shore waterways so I would chill the foot and not bleed out. My wife and I were traveling in sunny but icy weather in New York on Interstate 81 between Scranton and Binghamton and came upon a curvy hill and several cars were off to the side of the road. As I spoke aloud, "I wonder what—" Immediately, we spun around two times and stopped just before a guard rail. No big deal, eh? Yet, I thought where was the tractor trailer from over the hill that had only been seconds behind us? It somehow did not appear but it surely would have hit us, it may have slipped off just before the crest of the hill. We did not stick around to ponder the truck's ordeal but instead corrected our vehicle and drove off slowly for the sake of the ice.

Even as I wrote this chapter, I had a highway incident with a deer and impact that could have caused severe trouble or death had I just been one half second later. The actual strike was deadly to her but it was enough of a glancing blow that she only slammed the front, then side, with no loss of control to my car, or obliteration of the windshield, or the vehicle crashing. For certain God is in control!

To pretend that my life plan is simply lucky is incomprehensible. If this many blessings transpired by some unforeseen magic or sheer chance I would have to be the most auspicious person ever. If I believed my fortune was intrinsic or simple matter-of-fact luck, I would not be able to prevent the bonanza of money if I besieged a gambling establishment. It would be my duty to show off the "luck" if this was just happenstance. But it isn't just chance! I am surely not the only person to experience the watchful eye of our Savior. So many other stories and obvious miracles are occurring every day. Since I know the circumstances are a gift by a holy, graceful, and forgiving God, I can stand at the ready for anything.

To witness and experience truth first hand does grow faith. As it was said by the Lord's disciples written in (2nd Peter 1:16), "We have not followed cunningly devised fables when we made known unto you the *power* and coming of our Lord Christ Jesus, rather we were eyewitnesses of His majesty."

The facts are overwhelming and I am astounded how much mercy and unmerited grace I have been provided out of love alone. I think miracles should be praised, not made into a commonplace narrative for entertainment. The verdict in all of these cases is truth and intercession by my Savior. I trust that you too someday may grasp the glory of the one who provides miracles and see all He has done for you. I would hope you embrace the idea that miracles come from the provider, the same provider that gives us saving grace through the cross of Christ.

Chapter 6

Without Excuse!

I stood before a throne, and there was a judge too brilliant to gaze upon, and there was a hideous-looking creature to one side, almost human in stature, but dark and shrouded in what appeared to be like the covering of burnt feathers or wings. I swore I overheard someone mention, "Yes, he is the accuser!" I saw no jury, but there was another man to the side. He was shining and brilliant, and his body was certainly human, though his hands and feet had scars. There appeared to be witnesses all around me, but none were in sight; I just heard mumblings. Then I think I overheard the term "white throne," and someone announced that there would be a sentence passed at the end of the hearing. I was in somewhat of a fog but realized I had just been lying in the hospital, and the people all around me were talking anxiously, and then I heard a long, sustained beeeep. Then one of them said, "Mark it, the time is 11:47 am on Sunday the 5th of June."

Now a shiver and chill became so profound all over my body but it was not like a nervous affliction or fear and my body seemed so strange. I was no longer in my earthly body. Then came the clap of a gavel and without so much as split second the creature began prattling off a list of things so fast it was almost indistinguishable and yet they were things I recognized. It seemed impossible but in fact it was a list of every single time I broke the law and I do not mean the law of the land, this was a list of sins. "Oh my God," I thought, "this was the judgment seat!" This was becoming so overwhelming and daunting! I pondered, "Who is this thing they call the accuser? He is relentless and has not stopped for an instant; does he even breathe?" I could not stand this I need to speak up. I have to speak up. I shouted, "No, stop!" The thing ceased for a moment from the onslaught of listing my transgressions.

I fell to my knees and proclaimed, "I was not that bad, in fact I did some wonderful things, there were so many people who were murderers, thieves, so many were monsters who killed nations of people, why am *I* going through this ordeal?" I thought for a moment and screamed, "I was a good man, I know I went to church some, and I gave things to people, I was religious, I even believed in God." Just then; the figure to the right spoke, sounding as if there were tears in his voice; he uttered only a few words, he said, "I never knew you!" With that proclamation the ugly creature began even louder than before to rant insults in between each trespass and to roar at a more tumultuous pace to shout out my iniquities. It seemed now this was real and I was going to be found guilty, I had no representation ... this could not be a court of law or a fair hearing, what was going on?

It was then that I realized with a more consuming fear than ever before, I had heard it all. I had remembered friends and preachers, priests, and even the fakes and crazy folks on television. I had actually heard them say, "For the accuser of the brethren is cast down, which accused them before our God, day and Night" (Revelation 10:12). I knew there would be a hearing when John said in the book of Revelation, "then I saw a great white throne!" (Revelation 20:11–15). I also remembered the apostle Paul, saying "so then every one of us will give an account" (Romans 14:12).

I realized it so starkly at this moment, there was in fact, nothing in wait for those who ignored righteousness, nothing but death. The truth was in my mind but how could it be? I had not memorized the scripture. I had heard them, most of them more than once and ignored them; I figured they certainly could not be meant for me. I had believed the fashionable ideas of what a god should be; but this was real. Yes now they all came flooding in, all the condemnations were here! So many more verses assembled in my mind totally clear and convincing.

- ... thrown into the fire ... (Matt. 3:10)
- ... judgment and the fire of hell ... (Matt. 5:22)
- ... condemned to hell ... (Matt. 23:33)
- ... weeping and gnashing of teeth ... (Matt. 25:28–30)

- ... they will go away to eternal punishment ... but the righteous to eternal life ... (Matt. 25:31–46)
- ... unless you repent you will perish ... (Luke 13:3–5)
- ... he will judge men's secrets ... (Romans 2:16)
- ... you must be born again ... (John 3:3)
- ... whoever believes in him is not condemned, but those who have not are condemned already (John 3:17–18)
- ... Christ (He) put away sin by the sacrifice of Himself ... for it is appointed to men to *die once* and then the judgment .... (Heb. 9:27)

I was having those fatal verses bombard me as quickly as the thing would accuse me. I wish it would be like an injury or bruise on earth and I might become numb. Instead, this just got worse and worse, the pain was beyond any description and completely engrossing. I could not contain my crying and I even began to grit my teeth in anger, why was I not told? Woefully now, what I completely realized was that I had been told!

Then the *word* appeared so obvious as to why my representation kept so silent except for that one utterance. He spoke the only words he could say, "I never knew you," this was exactly what I was cautioned about on earth when those friends told me about the Gospel and I only replied, "I am good." Being good was not being saved. They said I might hear those exact words in the Bible found in Matthew 7:21. The lamb of God would only respond blankly towards any attempt to vindicate our sins through the declaration of our deeds, as if it could be payment.

Why didn't God try harder to convince me, but that answer was easy also? I knew it was my free will which now had condemned me. "Jesus" was on the lips of those who tried to love me and mocking was in my heart at their simple minded faith. I even now heard another verse in my soul from Second Peter, chapter three and verse nine, it was obvious God had tried to the greatest degree and I had rejected a savior. I heard, "The lord is not slack in keeping his promise as some count slowness, but He is patient toward all of us wanting *none* to perish, but for *all* to come to repentance" (II Peter 3:9). He had done everything possible to provide the Gospel to me. This was not about how good I thought I had been; this was about a choice. This was about denying Christ as the only saving truth.

It had also been explained to me so feverishly that repentance was *not about sorrow,* we are all sorry once we are caught and in line for punishment, rather repentance is a turning away from idols, dead works, and deeds which we hope to use as persuasion for forgiveness. The idea of an impossible compensation is what my friends meant when they told me that *grace* was the only way to be forgiven, not works, not an afterlife cleansing, and they assured me that purgatory was a myth, never to be found anywhere in God's word.

That monstrous thing would not stop and now it spat and drooled, the speed of this accusative torment was far beyond my understanding. Still no word was spoken from the throne or bright light behind the gavel and bench. No word from the Savior, he sat there only sobbing and distraught. His work, pain, and death resulted in nothing towards me, even though His words on the cross were, *"IT IS FINISHED."* I never received it. My name must have been blotted out of the Lamb's book of life (Revelation 13:8 and 21:27). The words in the Bible were true, now they arrived to me as if they had been inscribed in my head; oh God, if only they had been etched in my heart.

I knew it was over and my destiny forever was going to be horrid, disgusting, graphic, putrid, contemptible, and simply sad. I sprang up from my knees screaming, "It has to be a mistake, I cannot go to hell and this must be a mistake!" "Please, please don't let this happen," I bellowed.

The light from beyond the bench grew even stronger now and the brightness did not even make sense. It was if I had no eyes to see, but the light grew stronger and then it struck like a bolt of lightening right through me and it burned, it burned, and it burned. "This must be what electricity does to you as it passes through you," I murmured. Now it hurt so severely I could not even speak or scream. Then the light stopped and the pain was decreased ever so slightly. The sharp pain was now directly on my heart alone ... but it was less intense and it seemed to feel like a shock or electrical household current and I had felt that before. What was happening to me now? Once more it flashed into my body but this was somehow different, it was ... my real my body and it now felt similar to my earthly experiences, and once again, *zap*, the shock came.

The voices around me were no longer the trial witnesses, the Savior was not seated at the side sobbing and the vicious monster was not there shouting about my sinful frailties. Two of the people here were dressed in white; but no ... this was not the place where I had just been, this was instead, the hospital. I could distinctly hear one of them say, "No need for the paddles again; he has responded." That sweet pulsing beat, the beeping of the heart rate monitor, this was making me cry with such inundation. I was not far away from earth and the hospital, but rather I was still here on earth. Oh Lord, thank you!

How could I have missed it, why had I fought so hard before to ignore this love, the Bible feverishly tells me there is *no excuse!* (Romans 1:20–28) (John 15:22). I think the only question left, was would I respond to the one thing that lasts forever or would I go on with no hope, knowing certainly now, that I was worth another try.

Unconditional Love is not saving Grace!

Unconditional love: this expression is misused so often that it must be explained! Can you imagine if you lived many years, and you experienced some joyous or pleasurable moments, but for the most part you had an average or maybe even a less than average life? This was a life filled with some incredible joy but predominantly average or normal. There were of course, trials, some very moving difficulties, and even some devastating disappointments, only to discover when life ended it came to a ghastly, harsh, but unconditional tragedy. Most people think and even profess they believe the afterlife will be peaceful regardless of what has happens in this life. As if we are owed something! Most people would expect to go on into another life of ease, comfort, and no difficulty, correct? How overwhelming it would be to realize, you have died, you missed the gift of eternal life, you are not bound for heaven, and this reality is *unconditional*.

Let's consider the word that I just used, unconditional, and you will find most every person who says they "believe" will also state that God loves us unconditionally. Unconditional, yes, the love is unconditional, but our destiny is not based on this truth. Althoug God's love is unconditional, we need to comprehend that the promises of God always have a condition. The question we must face is why some of us stand toe to toe with the almighty and place "conditions" on our love returned? Without question many people unashamedly tell God, "I will not love you if your plan requires a Savior, or has only One God, or has just a single path, or maybe they roar, "You must love us no matter what we do!" You see the problem with the concept of unconditional love is that most of us do not understand what that means in regards to a formula of perfection. When discerning our own lives, we dare not disregard or ignore the concept of sin and the impact it has on our lives.

God is perfect; his standards are perfect, and He is completely perfect. He is perfect in not only *love,* but also *justice,* thus his love cannot be a lie. He must be just, and if he loves us unconditionally, then his forgiveness must have a *just* design, or He is a liar! It would be ludicrous to think God is at fault if our lives end in a harrowing conclusion forever away from Him. The fact of forgiveness and gift of grace is absolutely God's plan for everyone, and a plan where we are given free will and a freedom of choice that determines our destiny. Unconditional love is exactly that which God has for us, but that love alone is not able to *save us from our sins*. Only grace from the cross of Christ can erase sins, or we will perish, no matter how much we are loved. The Bible is precise (see: John 14:6, John 3:3, John 3:16–18, Romans 3:23–26, John 10:9, John 17:3, Acts 4:12). Not just this small list just mentioned, but in all of God's word, we are cautioned that we will perish if not saved.

You see, God proclaims that He is in turmoil and suffering at the highest degree to be certain that information about that gift of redemption is provided to all people (see II Peter 3:9). An endless flow and actual bombardment of awareness is being given to every person. God spoke clearly in Christ when he told the apostles about the reason for parable and soliloquy (see Matthew Chapter 13 and Luke 8:4–21). The mechanism behind parables is so that those who want the truth and open their heart will receive, and others will simply hear a story. Jesus went on to illustrate that every person is given the truth but many people are of such unreceptive soil that seeds cannot ever grow to the knowledge of redemption.

The Lord revealed many souls are like concrete or stone and the seeds will never take, others are like soil that only lasts a short time, and some allow seeds to be blown away or snatched and eaten by the birds. He continues to disclose that others are like a fertile soil but the growth does not last, some understand and are happy to know salvation but eventually deny it and walk away, and thankfully then … some of us will receive grace unto permanence.

This is what God does to give every person on this planet a chance, the Holy Spirit is God and knows every circumstance, and he leads us to understanding through seeds. God loves all of us (unconditionally) but not all of us are willing to receive the seeds and allow growth unto salvation though Jesus.

So it can be deduced that the word unconditional is not just inaccurate to apply to God's grace; rather, it is confrontational. Claiming that God must love us unconditionally unto salvation is a shameful, wayward challenge to make God fit the lives we lead. The love of God is unconditional and has no bounds, limits, or conditions; no not one. With contemplation of scripture we will find that the gift of salvation is offered freely and enthusiastically but if we revolt and try to make redemption a way of deeds or action and not a gift, then we are placing the condition on God himself. If someone attempts to gain access to God's home through any other means than a gift, then they will be the culprit that allowed eternal life to be stolen. The person that denies salvation through the grace of the cross will find themselves in the immutable predicament of being a sinner, with no Savior.

So, please receive that unconditional love and relax in his joy, but do not ignore that ever glorious call of the Holy Spirit. It would be magnificent if you would actively seek to be born again, from above, through Christ. There is no condition for God's love through God himself; there is only the condition of a rebellious nature by those who deny the Savior, which will lead to an ill-fated death.

To ignore the gift of Christ; would equate to a life where you experienced a few joyous or pleasurable moments, had an average or less than average life, experienced many trials, some very moving difficulties, and even some devastating disappointments, only to discover it has, in fact, come to a ghastly, harsh, and unconditional tragic outcome.

Endless resource!

I know that none of us want to admit we don't know it all! I joke about that but know that many of us have a strong aversion to learning things which challenge our balance *if* we think the conclusion is already a given. So it is possible then, we feel that we must already have the answer to the eternal question, because God would not leave that to chance. What this supposition fails to do is know that unconditional love is not just a term, but actual love requires the most intense balance of cultivation and free will. We have essentially been given exactly what we desire regarding the things of the spirit.

The Lord is pouring out information to you every day regarding the Gospel. Some of us simply choose to ignore it. Incredibly enough, most people choose to vehemently ignore the good news because it does not compliment them. I would pray that no one is going to let the single sin of pride (blaspheme), prevent them from going the distance and then end up having a stubborn free will land them in endless separation. I cannot speculate on the hurdle that might be facing someone before making a decision and committing to our Savior because there is an endless array of great writing and of course there is the Holy Bible. There are so many dozens of writings that prove the veracity of Christ. Hurdles are tough enough for anyone to overcome. However, I suggest that you go after it!

Many strong Resources!

If there is interest; then here are some resilient books of inspiration which carry strength and potency. One of the most comforting books for the person struggling with the premise that knowledge or intelligence is something that defies spirituality and you believe it might prevent you from understanding the true nature of the Lord, then you probably want to try *More Than a Carpenter*, by Josh McDowell. This reveals a staunch non-believer of great intelligence starting out to prove the lie of Christianity. Of course, God chose differently. Another such intricate book of the same venue is *Mere Christianity* by the famed C.S. Lewis, who is also the writer of the famous collection of Narnia tales. These men are men of incredible intellect and very sound thinkers of our era and yet they discovered the love via the truth of the Gospel.

If you are seeking a stunning depiction of all that surrounds us in our natural and developed world which shows or proves the evocation of God, then you should try the *Signature of God* by Grant R. Jeffrey. The depth of archeological, physical, natural, and biblical confirmation is astounding, interesting, enlightening, and beautiful.

To find an author who is well experienced in drawing people to salvation and showing the kindness which can bring them closer, then you should read Billy Graham's *Storm Warning*. All the conclusions about modern day calamities, whether changes, hearts of terrorists, and hearts of the subdued is consistent with a man who has traveled the globe seeking peace, to love his fellow man and give him fair Biblical warning. Graham's other works are also quite heartwarming and bountiful with information and devotion towards all people of this world.

For the beloved descendants of God's chosen race; read this heart wrenching story about family and change, then you probably will cry and surely will be moved while reading *Betrayed* by Stan Telchin. This is story all about the family feelings when they discover a child who seems to have betrayed them. This gives you a deep understanding of what can happen when someone really risks it all to go the distance to find the truth. The turmoil from her family is understandably rampant while some of the responses seem out of bounds from any reasonable reaction, but the conclusion is so very heartwarming.

A desire to know the enormous sacrifice and profound degree of reconciliation that God provided through the

Worth Another Try

solution of grace would be *The Grace Awakening*, by Charles R. Swindoll. In this, you will discover the monumental difference between the cost of the gift which God gives us and the concept of earning forgiveness. You will come to recognize that we could not cover our transgressions with our deeds, when the blood of the Lamb is the real elucidation.

If anyone has ever battled with the idea of being saved for certain by the loving gift of grace alone, they would do well to be consoled by *Saved Without a Doubt*, by John MacArthur Jr. This work contains remarkable Biblical conviction to support the basis of a loving grace that keeps you in God's hand regardless of the frailty of our feelings.

I imagine some people might already know the great teacher, preacher, and kind gentleman, Charles Stanley. If you have ever listened to him in televised sessions, you most likely know the genuine nature of a giving soul. If you have not had the pleasure, please be assured of his honesty and relatable grasp of the Word of God! He has provided so much information in the form of loving exposition. These expository works are quite numerous but my favorite is *The Reason for My Hope*. Hope is something we all have but Stanley gives the finest explanation of how to put it into action and why the greatest hope lies within God.

I have listed here some written works which have a very specific purpose for one's edification. My reason was an attempt to show that discernment is up to *each individual!* We will have no excuse when we stand before an almighty God. It is out there in our reach and we cannot avoid the love of God. His love desires us to feed and absorb the seeds of legitimate salvation and righteousness. That does not mean he wants robots to snap to attention in obedience. Force is not even a question in this mixture. Righteousness is not a formula derived by our actions versus our transgressions; instead it is coming to know the forgiveness that God has earned for us by His sacrificial action. Thus the Lord eagerly wants us to know that He has fixed the one problem we could never solve. He has provided a gift and sacrifice that meets the perfect standards of a perfect God.

There is cavalcade of writing about spirituality, religion, and theology, and perhaps confusion is possible, but conclusively the Lord has placed the actual good news before us. I hope I have invited you to seek the Gospel, which is a gift of love that will give us something forever. If we shrink at the idea of God being the *do all, tell all,* and *be all* when it comes to enjoying His gracious company forever, then we cannot blame anyone else if we come to an end without His redemption. We need to step up to the truth, say yes, and commit, because there is *no excuse* for not knowing the Gospel and what is meant by salvation through the gift of *grace alone!*

Chapter 7

Is The Word of Grace Enough?

"In the beginning was the Word and the Word was with God and the Word was God" (John 1:1). There is almost no other verse in the Bible that is quite as succinct in describing the trustworthiness of the Lord. If the Word has been shared with us through the prophets, then how credible would it be if the Word dwelt amongst us? We can depend on the inexorable cohesion that God has planned for those who want to be with him, especially if he would come and be human for the reason of cleansing, communicating, saving, and loving us. There are many people that think that God has in fact used prophets to explain or convey ideas toward mankind. This Gospel book by John goes on to state that the Word came to dwell amongst us and became flesh! (John 1:14). That being said, what if the very Word itself did become a walking being, how much faith would you put into the Word?

I earnestly pray that you would consider it. God walking on earth would undoubtedly be the most trustworthy method of conveyance of any message or execution of deed. That is exactly what happened. It was essential for the validity of a supernatural sacrifice to be perfect, blameless, without blemish, and eternal so it could encompass every soul in the earth, thus it needed to be Christ and Christ needs to be God, incarnate! This was even a bone of contention at that time he lived and continues to impede some people from believing, naturally he was accused of blaspheme and threats of stoning were common towards him in his three-year ministry. If a sacrifice is meant for every human soul and meant to be of eternal value, it has to be God Himself as the provision.

This following statement was one of many that made people consider the possibility and reality of a visit from the almighty, he said: "I and the Father are *One*" (John 10:30). Christ was also quoted as saying; "I am the resurrection and the life," (John 11:25), immediately before raising a friend who had been four days deceased. Jesus also said: "Even though you do not believe me, believe the works, so that you might know and understand that the Father is in me and I am in the Father" (John 10:37–38). When he spoke to the ill and infirmed and He proclaimed, "Your sins are forgiven!" he explained to those around him the reason for these words rather than saying "walk and rise" (Luke 5:23, Matthew 9:1–8). It was to reveal that He in fact has the power for forgiveness of sin. At this declaration the witnesses were screaming about blaspheme. The learned teachers and scribes of the time were completely correct in the assessment that *only God can forgive sin*. The only oversight at that time was that they did not recognize the Messiah or the reason that an *eternal* cleansing required that He be the Son of God.

The miracles of feeding families, preaching perfect peace, healing the sick and forgiving sin were just a precursor to the event yet to come. He would show the world that eternal sacrifice provides a monumental peace. He would prove the glory of what Jehovah had been teaching the Hebrews for centuries. "Without the shedding of blood there is no forgiveness" (Hebrews 9:22). Very simply ask yourself, who could be worthy of a single sacrifice that would forgive all of Mankind itself, other than God Himself.

If you have a barrier to understanding or believing the uniqueness of Christianity versus other theologies or ideologies, then I invite you to dedicate time in the concentrated study of all major religions and the unique one called Christianity. Fourteen years and thousands of hours devoted to that very studied resulted in a book called, "One Lord, Many Ministries." The book was an attempt to reveal very intricate and inspiring comparisons of the major theologies and the only one which is based *solely on grace*. All the arduous collations were from the religious books and history of what each of these religions claim to be its foundation, and also, the origin or the life blood concepts that each of them are trying to ferry to the recipient.

All religions but one tell us that we need to perform some behavior, to make some *god,* do something because of those actions. Alas, the difference and singularity of Christianity is discovered only if you spend the time reading the message of Jesus. Then you will discover it is about a salvation mission that *had* to be done to provide redemption for all our race of humans. While every other religion is developed on a hypothesis of our actions working towards an end; one, and only one religion, is strictly based on *receiving a gift,* a gift of such enormous glory, performed by one Holy individual. All other beliefs are an attempt to rectify our condition to a degree of acceptable behavior or a reasonably defensible dimension.

If we form a postulation of labor based restitution, it fails to provide absolute legitimacy. This becomes just a hobbling attempt to uplift our own miserable bankruptcy. We need to recall God's standard of "eternal" sacrifice is perfect. If we as humans have willfully sinned against God, it is rather contemptible to set some goal of duties which would rejuvenate us to wholeness. I am a believer of (Christ) the love of God, and still every day sin happens, I fail towards God and my fellow man with regularity. I could never reach a point of reconciliation in terms of deed or work-based deliverance. No one can do that!

It is error to propose we are beings of infinite goodness upon birth. There is no evidence of such a spirit or norm in human behavior rather we need to be taught to be kind and selfless. We are filled with love by our creator and mimic that very acutely, this is true, but we also gravitate towards sinfulness by inheritance (Psalms 58:3, Job 25:4, Ephesians 2:3, Romans 3:10–12, Romans 3:23, Romans 5:18–19). Wanting our own desires without respect to the possibility of offending God or others is not only inborn but has become fashionable to most all of the world's elite inhabitants. By this, we unashamedly introduce a set of prescriptions that will excuse our performance and supposedly mend our relation with the almighty. Then, it seems we mortals slap a title on it and it passes for what we call religion. What we really want is not the forgiveness of sin; instead it is to be perceived as being OK in the viewpoint of the common person by our stance in religion. That is the modus operandi of all humans when we are left unrestrained; we want our appraisal to be relative goodness.

Mother Teresa pointed out the turmoil that faces the oppressed and accurately said, "it is so very difficult to discuss sinfulness on an empty stomach." I believe once we have gotten even the slightest degree of comfort to satisfy our flesh, it is quite depressing how we reveal our true nature. Unlike the destitute, I have never heard of a toddler or young one (born of means) who is screaming or crying at the top of his lungs so he can have something, and then, suddenly he discerns those actions are all about self interest and nothing less, and then he excuses himself for the calamity that people are witnessing. On the contrary, if children do anything they begin to *explain* why they believe they have a "need" or why they "want" even when, or most commonly when, it is not legitimate.

Once we have tasted the reassurance of substance as we grow, we are so directed towards our own wants that we cannot even reflect or reason that we need to judge ourselves to a *Holy God* regarding sin or disobedience. Instead, we just make excuses or cast blame or seek an "I'll deal with it later," cleansing place as our destiny. A review of the book of Genesis in the very beginning of the fall of mankind will show that is exactly how the first humans reacted to God when they were told they had disobeyed and sinned. Girl blames snake, boy blames girl, and snake laughs and thinks, "Yep, all I did was tell them that they had *not gotten the best* from God, and it was believed!'

That is where humankind fails so fatally back then and right up to this very day. We have now been given perfect salvation through Christ and the most enduring gift and flawless solution to a problem we could never solve ... and yet most people do not want to believe. So, to this very day we are given grace through the Son of God, simple and permanent, and some of us still turn to the snake and ask, "Is this really the truth?" We also ask, "Is this the best way for us to get what *we* want?" We even go so far as to think, "Is God the Son the only way to receive reconciliation from God?"

For certain with this technique of circumvention towards sinfulness, we could inevitably miss true restitution! The horrifying picture is that we are only truly in love with God if we unite with him by *free will*. Thus, "Faith comes by hearing, and hearing by the Word of God" (Romans 10:17). Are you listening?

We witness the scriptural result from the very first beings created by the Lord. They doubted God's best plan and thus they did the only thing that could cause a gap or breakage between themselves and God. In essence, they took free will and called God a liar. They chose forbidden fruit as if it was something that would create a better situation or that it was some treasure that the Lord had denied them. They believed they could be equal to God in some respect; they felt they had not been given the best that could ever be offered. Even if you take the creation story as an anecdote and not face value, the premise is loud and clear; although face value is what the Lord would have us believe. The insult was the greatest of any sin, it was the sin of pride. Do we not do that today by rejecting the simplicity and purity of God's sacrifice as "Enough?" Dare we tell God, his truth is not genuine, should we blame him for our free will when we reject the glory of His plan through the Messiah verses our doubting conscience. When Christ said, "first we must become like children," (Matt 18,3–5) it was clear that the factor of trust in the Father was the concept being offered.

That today is where the line is drawn regarding the redemption plan of God. Many people think they do not need it, some think it could never be that simple, others will blatantly reject it by continuing to offer works or tasks to build a tower of merit to reach *a god*. All these stances will end in the destruction of a relationship, because we take free will and leave our destiny to chance or to some conglomeration of polytheism or we try to blame God by never considering the need for a change in respect to our sinfulness.

The need for salvation is not a decision of where we want to go, or how we wish to be judged in respect to the world's opinions; rather, it is a choice of whether we want to be with God and live in His glory. If the notion of an afterlife and present life association is based on hoping we pass the test of deeds, or that we meet a standard, we are obviously attempting to throw any liability of indictment into the hands of God. Think that over and it will be evident that if we are not actively seeking a relationship or completely confident that we are free from any hindrance of sin, then we are stagnant or we are not authentically looking for closure on the subject of everlasting *spotlessness*. God tells us that the blood of Christ will make us incorruptible (Romans 2:7, II Corinthians 5:2–4, I Corinthians 15:52).

The flood of scripture that points to Christ as the lamb that was slain for all, whom God loves, is incalculable, and it is present and available for most anyone. If the seeds of the Gospel are planted in you and you reject them, who can you blame? The comprehension and fidelity to this fact is up to us! So do not believe any imaginary dark monster or serpent or ideas that can actually stand in the way. The resolute will call Christ into their hearts and receive the endowment of assurance and it is precisely that, a promise which will be honored forever. That faith will grant you the certainty to be with Him forever, because no sin can cause the sting of death, if you choose life eternal. One of the most important statements spoken by Jesus was this, in response to Martha when he knew he was going to raise her brother from the dead right on the spot. He said, "*I am* the resurrection and the life." "He who believes in me *will live*, even though he dies; and whoever lives and believes in me will never die. Do you believe this?" "Yes Lord," she told him, "I believe that you are the Christ, Son of God, who has come into the world" (John 11:25–27).

A transformation of this kind, will secure your name in the lamb's book of life, it is one that takes faith. Faith in the simple gift of salvation, purchased through the blood sacrifice that was Christ himself. Any person can be born again by the true reflection and commitment to Christ. If this happens to you the Bible tells us the Holy Spirit will be the sealer of your faith and you will have been bought as a disciple of the Lord. After that, if you find yourself doubting the simplicity and resolve, that is normal with any real transition. However, if you find yourself rejecting Jesus and become apostate, once again claiming some form of merit based absolution, you either need to quiet your soul with the *Word* of God or you may realize you never truthfully made a choice for freedom from sin.

This brings us to closure regarding the idea of trusting the Word of God. He who walked and talked, died and rose, and was not a philosopher, nor trendsetter, nor a common world figure for us to mimic, nor a simple teacher, but instead he is the anointed one, the Lamb of God, the Messiah, the Christ. If the

Word on earth and in heaven and in your heart is the best plan, then you have found substantiation in the one who is almighty.

Beware though, there is in fact a roaring lion, fallen angel, and figure in the world that wars against you from understanding and commitment, but the Bible tells us Satan cannot overcome the believer if they are saved by Christ. "Greater is He that is in you, than he that is in the world," (John 4:4). "If God is for us who can be against us," (Romans 8:31)? "No weapon formed against you will prosper," (Isaiah 54:17). If God, in action, love, sacrifice, hope and eternal affection are not enough for you, maybe you have no real desire for truth.

However, I believe the Bible clearly declares that turning away from the salvation plan of the almighty will unconditionally end in a life forever separated by sin. Do not take my word. Go look at these words ... the *Word* dwelt amongst us, He is enough, and His reason for coming was eternal salvation. The symbolic past with the blood of goats, birds, bulls, and animals cannot compare to "sinless blood" and only God is sinless. The Lord overcame death and sin.

- The penalty for sin is death (Romans 6:23).
- The first of sin came / death [Adam and Eve disobey] (Genesis 3:1–24) (Romans 5:12).
- We are separated from God by sin and need salvation (Isaiah 59:2)

- The shedding of Christ's blood offers eternal redemption (Leviticus 17:11, Exodus 24:8, Revelation 12:11, Genesis 15:9–17, Psalm 51:16–17, Genesis 3:15).
- God's own arm and God's own righteousness "worked salvation" by destroying sin, not just a *cover* (Isaiah 59:15–16).

To reject deliverance from sin, through the work of the cross of Christ, and hope to replace that with our own feeble acts of reconciliation is not the act of a contrite heart or broken spirit. To consider or think that "anything is better than the incarnation of Our Lord, or the sacrificial offering, or His forgiveness" is no way to respond to the Holy of Holies. If Jesus still appears to you, to not be the *Word* of God, and compassion does not represent the perfect gift, then we all must remain as broken sin filled beings.

"We are all unclean, and our *deeds* are like filthy rags," compared to the Lamb, (Isaiah 64:6). I know that the *Word is enough* and that grace means giving the glory to God and contrition means fearing the Lord, and rejoicing comes from His eternal mercy through "Christ himself," not through our worthless attempts to cover up our dirt.

Chapter 8

The Final Question

I have experienced such wonderful awareness as a son, friend, brother, husband, and father. When I think of *father*, I think of a term that portrays a gracious, caring, stern, and yet gentle nature. That is because my earthly father and my father in heaven have those very traits. My beloved Dad is now in heaven and lives with his best friend, the one who gave him all those qualities.

The nature of caring and the nature of firm regard run hand and hand but they sometime appear to be at ends with each other. On the one hand you know certain absolutes which you want to convey with emphasis, on the other hand you want to offer them with kindness and gentleness. If those absolutes are contrary to the widespread general perception you are presented with a dilemma. With children at a very young age there is a much overused example but nevertheless it is exact, you tell the small ones, "Don't play in the street or you could be hit by a car." As the young ones grow older you find the ideas about caution are less black and white but some do remain perfect in content and certainty, regardless of the common viewpoint.

Some of the most profound ideas which remain precise forever are some like, "Do unto others as you would have them do unto you." Another saying is, "Say your prayers." Another is, "God is love," but dare we risk the chance to misconstrue that notion, we may have our loved ones thinking anything lovely must be God. Still another example of a confusing saying is, "All good children go to heaven," which might have been said to comfort children, but think about those children who grew to be monsters and campaigned to do incomparable destruction to others as they got older. Do these onetime children warrant heaven simply because they were good in their youth? The point is that some things we believe to be absolute are in fact not sure in the very least.

As a father the task of teaching is no way an easy one, because you have so many notions that eventually are proven false or have been misrepresented by the generations. A father is sought after for accurate and wise guidance and in cases of danger you are looked to for precision or the consequence can even be fatal in some respects. It can be fatal to the soul, mind, and even the body. Thus you must have the aforementioned discerning characteristics to present the truth or a huge error hangs in the balance. To answer a question of finality it must require evidence and sound judgment so that it can be presented with confidence of understanding.

Father God has provided us a most perfect approach to be infused with him in an intimate way and be assured of that continuance. That way is to be freed from sin. If we are freed completely freed from sin, we can be in his eternal home and even be involved with him deeply while we are here on earth. So, our heavenly Father needs to communicate to us the exact way of making that relationship work. Like any relationship that is to be united for the duration, the giver of knowledge must allow free will in the pupil. Sometimes the only method of instruction is letting one see others and the circumstance they have experienced.

Belief through Experience

I have witnessed and heard of many fascinating accounts of faith and sturdy resilience by those who were involved. One of the first such stories that comes to mind is about a visitor to my church from the foreign missions in the Amazon area in South America. As you can imagine the facilities and desolate surroundings are trying enough but to have to relate the Gospel to people of such a different background is sometimes impossible. It seems this missionary was living with one tribe of native people who had little interaction with outsiders or to be perfectly frank they knew little of any other race or anything other than their own environment.

For a long time the clan of people tolerated this very dear woman who incidentally developed every sickness you can imagine. She also had no contact with others outside of these new friends, except an occasional supply plane which would land miles away that would come every 90 days. She was faced with such an impossible task of communicating the Gospel because she had to use the Bible. These people had no written language. Almost twelve years passed while she plodded along attempting to give these friends the good news of Jesus. She had barely reached one third of them, and the local medicine man was naturally a mortal enemy because much of the medicine (both corporeal and spiritual) would in fact be of great help, and many times prayer was the only factor, with nothing else to which the healing could be attributed.

The days were becoming so dreary and she felt she could never quite get to the others the words without using an established alphabet which she had developed for her committed students. You see they had survived with no formal way of expression through writing. They would actually communicate with carvings and scratches in large plant leaves. The Gospel was getting to some, and yet she thought there was no hope for the others. Her son had decided to join her for a stay and arrived on the next plane with a shipment of goods.

He had been hoping and praying earnestly for "Preacher Mom," a kind of nickname her friends had given her. Her son had felt some enlightenment and wanted to share an idea; it was a common one, and the letters she sent home had made him seek the guidance of the Holy Spirit. He suggested the old shock and awe method and said to use a modern technique. So after some work they developed the Gospel of John in the leaf orientation and they loaded up the mission supply plane and flew over the village (dropping LEAF leaflets literally) dropping the Gospel from the "big loud bird." The joy and excitement was so appealing and the success was brilliant and the word became something meaningful to them, because it was given in a form they could handle and appreciate. The numbers of believers doubled from this success, but so many still thought the message was a hoax. Both she and her son were so saddened by the lack of growth. The numbers of converted friends slowed between one half and two thirds of the group, and they thought they had run out of ideas. Fortunately, Bible believers such as these realize that there is *someone* who is never out of ideas.

When we become ultimately discouraged, there is always some great plan known to the Almighty. The next circumstance would be their reward for being patient and faithful for so long. With great news and free will hanging in the balance, her son stayed on for a bit of time and praise God that he chose to stay. It would be that decision that would allow God's glory to be seen.

The following week one of the young boys disobeyed his father and all of the tribe's leaders and went for a swim. He did it in a place known by the tribal residents, to the best of translations, as Caiman alley. It was a part of the river which is so infested with these black alligators that no one had *ever* survived the area or made it to the island across this stretch of river.

Worth Another Try

They literally had so many deaths it had become an absolute off limits place. The missionary had seen these men fight off jaguars and tackle anacondas, even though the tribesman were very brave, entering this water area was not even a consideration to them. The scene with this boy was frantic and *all* of the men would by no means enter the water. The young missionary man thought, "How could they be so afraid?" Dreadfully, at the moment of this tragic crisis with this young boy, "Preacher Mom" was not on site, and her son could not understand why there was such hesitancy from all the men, since the swim seemed so short.

He tried desperately to communicate but all he saw was panic and could not get any answers or adequately understand the language. So, he threw off any thought of self, even while some men were trying to drag him back. He dove in and swam furiously to the other side and grabbed the young lad. He started back, boy in tow, and could not understand why all the men were frozen with fear on the other side with spears and waiting anxiously. The entire ordeal seemed to happen in a split second, but really was several minutes. The mission preacher's son swam back with the boy to an accolade of cheers and he was swarmed by delight from the father and mother and many others. He did not have a clue what was happening, he thought, "Maybe none of them can swim?"

To his astonishment, only moments later, it was then explained to him about the reptilian danger and certain deadly peril. This explanation came only after one of the women had

The Final Question

gone and gotten his mom, and she revealed the fearful issue once she arrived at the location. The men began pointing out the extreme number of gator-like creatures across the water on the banks and even then some still swirling about. This phenomenal rescue was not just an incidental possibility, but rather a miracle. God planned that the young man would stay longer, and it was just what the doctor ordered. Not the medicine man ... but the healer of all mankind.

Still this was not the greatest miracle witnessed by these beloved people; rather that event was yet to come. You see after twelve years of intense work and arduous waiting, "Preacher Mom" was about to experience the exhilaration of joy and grace from God, once again. There was a stirring amongst the men. In the next week the tribe kept discussing "others" existing about four miles from the village. The people here had never met the people there, but many were growing more inquisitive with ever increasing sightings, so the leader of the "scouts," a name in their tongue they had given the curious men, decided they would take a party of men to investigate.

The group boarded their river vessels and traveled down the river to an embankment and shore where they had never visited before and sure enough found the other village. After a period of uncertainty, peaceful curiosity, and some hesitancy at the shore, they found a similar way of communication to those whom they just met, maybe a long lost cousin, per chance! The group was still not sure how welcome they were, yet it seems this new tribe was so anxious to convey a story from their spiritual leader, the medicine man, who had been dealing with a vision regarding visitors, which he had been pondering for months. This medicine man had acted upon the vision and idea and now invited the newcomers to see what he had for them. They were all a bit skeptical and hesitant, including "Preacher Mom" and her son, but everyone followed cautiously as they were led into the center of the village, where they found a standing structure.

It was incredible and stunning to the eyewitnesses! The place had seating and benches all across, all of which were pointing to the front, where there was another structure much like a table or podium. These "new friends" had not heard the Gospel stories, but still, they had built a pulpit-like stand. However, the most astonishing spectacle was on the outside of the hut on the roof; a set of two sticks wrapped in twine and lashed together stood there. It stood at the top of the hut, in front at the peak, and was inexplicably a *cross* atop the structure. The medicine man claimed the vision would not let go of him, and he was convinced someone would come to explain.

In the weeks to follow, the friendships grew, and the vision of the good news and a new life had become a reality. The new tribe was so receptive and welcomed the Gospel and saving grace of our Lord, nearly every member of this new group was won over by the joy of the Lord. This took place in virtually no time at all [a couple of months], but nothing compared to the twelve years spent with the other tribe. The overwhelming elation of both the Mom and Son was well worth all the faithful burdensome years of time serving the Lord. "There is joy before the angels of God, over (even) one sinner who repents," (Luke, 15:10).

This kind of miracle, to see so many receive the message of Jesus as Savior, is exciting. Our Father in heaven wants us to know him and be freed from sin. We do have free will to turn away from the great redeemer and ignore the good news of redemption, but if we do turn away, that only leaves us impoverished. So, being Father God involves loving and also giving ideas, warnings, and even eternal good news, but it is up to us to embrace the learning when the question is of such a critical nature.

Another Sunday, we had another missionary come to church to present his story, which was one of woe and recovery. He was from Germany and had just lost his beloved wife and daughter in a terrible fire. The story details he shared were not gruesome, and he did not dwell on the particulars of pain and suffering. He was so confident in the peace that they knew as believers, now in the presence of God. His resolve was amazing. He then went on to tell of another tragedy shortly after, in which his other daughter was lost to a drunken driving accident. Still, this man was so filled with joy and spoke so enthusiastically about the Gospel. I was stunned how fervently he remained in faith? He had lost three of the dearest people in his life in a matter of less than a year. He had a young boy and girl, as the remaining members of his family, whom he now had to rear without the kinship of the two eldest siblings and maternal partner.

The remarkable vision was seeing the glow and the true bliss in him when he spoke of winning souls in one of the most desperate of areas of our world when it seemed he should have been so veritably broken. All his family members were believers, so he was comforted to know they were immediately in the presence of the Lord after their earthly demise. (See II Corinthians 5:7–8). Fervent faith is what it takes to go on sharing the good news.

These circumstances had not impeded his plan to spread the word across some of the darkest parts of Germany still shrouded by the remnants of the Berlin Wall and the still-oppressive nature from the cold war. The places he would visit with the good news of Christ had for years separated families from each other, and still he was moving with the power of the Lord. His life was not destroyed, as the plan of Satan would have it, and his countenance was not grim like a stumbling block, but instead it was pushing forward and the love of Christ was eminently being shared. Just incredible!

Across our own nation and internationally a long time program exists that was founded by David Wilkerson. The life story of his own testimony can be found in the book, "The Cross and the Switchblade." I have many times first hand seen the miracle of transformation which has become the difference in men and their families and I have seen men and boys come to a tremendous victory in their lives through a program called Teen Challenge. This program has saved families and men because of only one thing. The program is designed not only to provide understanding about the slavery and devastation of substance abuse, but it also is designed to give permanence to that recovery. The governor of Connecticut was stupefied by the curriculum development, considering the comparison of other social programs especially those that were simply government run. The success rate for programs run by the state is usually around the single digit percentage, while the program success rate with Teen Challenge is over 80 percent for completion and no return. The Governor had only one thing to say, "The only difference I can conclusively see is the 'Jesus factor.'" When you have so much to live for and have been given a way to understand the eternal factors of life you find a way to believe the truth of the Gospel, here and forever. If you seek more information about this beautiful life saving program, you will come to realize how valuable we are to the Lord, "He, who the Son sets free, is free indeed." (John 8:36).

There are truly hundreds of personal stories I have either witnessed or read about which give faithful testimony to a life dedicated to the Savior. Faith comes by hearing of the Word! Jesus is the Word and answer to eternity. Faith is awesome to embrace. I think one of the best ways to describe faith would be, "I just know He is there!" If it helps to embrace that simplicity, there is a story that Billy Graham got from a child who told him how he knew that God was real. "Out of the mouth of babes!!" The young boy compared God to a kite and the certainty of knowing something is there. The boy said, "Even though it may get up beyond the clouds or fog or out of view, every once in a while, I feel the tug, and I know it is still there." I have also seen and read about the remarkable recovery technique that is being used in medicine. One such place is a clinic that has a Biblical approach. This clinic is lead by Doctor Mark Stengler and located in Encinitas, Ca. Doctor Stengler is a devout Christian and He has discovered techniques and processes that have increased the reversal of life ending diseases and saved many lives. The numbers and results are staggering to say the least. He employs the Naturopathic / Holistic and Biblical remedies found in Old Testament scripture combined with prayer. Recovery percentages for these patients are un-chartable. The success against disease that drugs have been unable to accomplish is compelling, with stories of other physicians simply calling these healings, miraculous! Patients have experienced the complete elimination of cancer, diabetes, MS, heart disease, migraines, and IBS. No conclusion I write here in a paragraph can completely convince you of God's desire to regain our souls and renew our faith. This needs to be seen to embrace its glorious validity, so go read more about the wonderful things the Lord has for us, if we trust and obey with the inception of salvation as the foundation.

    I imagine that even a waterfall of my own stories might not be convincing if someone does not place much importance in forgiveness or eternal grace. For the veracity of the Gospel a person must want the answer to the final question. I can corroborate that the Bible is the word of God. I have seen holy results based on the Bible truth. I ask you, "Don't you think faithful testimony is the way to touch the soul?"

I want to offer one thing for consideration when making a reasonable decision regarding the inevitability of a destiny with eternity. That one consideration, which is immutably certain, is that our *opinion* is not a viable notion when measuring our destiny. If God has a plan and His standard requires faultlessness, then we need to believe that singularity of His design. So many people have seen his goodness and yet they desire to make him out to be a schizophrenic! Any "god" that would theoretically present himself in so many confusing ways of a so-called "*achievement-based restitution*" and then, allow us to basically *guess* at our outcome regarding our afterlife, is a dangerous and untrustworthy spook, and no real god at all. It must be profusely clear that God *does not need our help* to save us, He already suffered the cross. Our deeds as an additional ingredient, or some down payment, or assistance to the truth of the grace of Jesus, is simply an appalling insult. I hope that is understood?

The authenticity of faith in the Gospel of Christ is the holiness, uniqueness, and the absoluteness and can be easily chosen if we actually want to be with God. If on the other hand, we seek to figure out some puzzle so some day we may boast about worthiness, then we are possibly doing exactly what Jesus warned us about. Not receiving Grace is actually idolatry. Making an icon or idol of our own actions, a temple of great worth by indulging in vagueness, or the mysterious, or intellect, or maybe the grand achievement of working it all out on our own; that too is idolatry! If we do so, don't we sidestep the inevitable that only God saves? It was no coincidence that the name given to the Messiah at birth was Yeshua, which means "God saves." Immanuel, the name also given to the Christ, means, "God with us." The story of Jesus is not a quaint bedtime legend or happy little Christmas fable. It is a story of God's way of forgiveness.

The Bible explains the unpardonable sin as the only thing God *cannot* forgive. Why is that unforgivable, because we would be demanding another plan with an *unqualified* savior! Contemplate this equation, it makes complete sense. Saying NO to forgiveness is unpardonable! The Gospels (Mark 3:28–30, Matt 12:31–32, and Luke 12:10) describe this most horrific sin and that action is to refuse the loving offer of Father God. That sinful action is to reject the wooing of the Holy Spirit and to ignore the calling of God, who asks us to choose and know the truth of salvation. That is blaspheming! If this is a persistent choice to abandon the sacrifice of God's own Son, then by the nature of free will it cannot be forgiven. If a person does not repent right up to their final hour in this world, then there is no more good news to consider and they have chosen separation and "no pardon." That is why it is unpardonable! Would you ever want to be guilty of that?

The glorious love of our Lord is worth meticulous pursuit. Remember to Him your value is *worth another try* and He is making all intercession that *you will allow*. He does not place

The Final Question

serious warnings and truth in our lives as though they were just suggestions. His Laws were never the Ten Recommendations! God's standard is flawlessness. His Gospel is not a social gospel of good tidings and giving it your best try with inspiring thoughts like "You can do it," "Go for it," "You can succeed," or "You can earn it." He is actually telling us that we cannot do it without Him. The gift of grace is free. He regularly gives us great news, but more importantly, like a good Father, He warns us of the consequence if we throw deliverance back in His face. The caution from our Lord about missing salvation; is a warning of lethal significance.

God's warnings are vitally important. Do you believe anyone would apply some form of relativism to a simple sign that was clear as day that would save you from mortal harm? No, you would never travel down the road and ignore a sign stating, "Dangerous curve: slow down or you will crash and DIE!" At this critical point, you would never consider opinions from your spouse, or a friend, or someone in the car, upon seeing that sign. You would never exclaim, "Oh that warning is to judgmental," or "It is not open-minded," or "That is not fair to everyone!" I doubt anyone would knowingly be that obtuse.

Why then would anyone adhere to the common idea of life after death as pure guesswork or just expect to someday to brag about a prize of heaven, to brag about our ticket to paradise, as if *we earned it,* rather than receiving the gift of forgiveness and resurrection from above? We are of far too much value and worth, a worth that needed the precision of God's best effort, and that was the cross.

God is not a cheerleader for our great deeds, regarding heavenly access! Rather, God has made it clear we cannot clean ourselves completely to meet His standards. He has done that through the cross. He gets the glory, not us! God has let us know He performed the only worthy redemptive power when He took our sins at the cross, forgave us, and rose from the dead. Every religion that claims cleansing or eternal life is earned through *our own deeds* is a counterfeit, claiming they are better than God's only Son.

If you want to be with God you need to love the plan that he made for forgiveness, otherwise you are telling the almighty, "My dutiful actions are more important than your Son's shed blood." A deeds based redemption is attempting to *make God a debtor*. It would be like saying, "God *you owe me heaven* because I, *not you,* did something worthy of eternal life."

We can undeniably conclude that we are valued, but there remains an unanswered final question, and it is an absolute one. It remains unanswered if you have not already called upon the name of Jesus for salvation. That question is: how will you receive a close, perfectly clean, and permanent holy relationship with God, one good enough to belong in his home forever? What is the answer? Only the *gift* of grace!

God wishes us in His presence forever but we must be sin free to meet that standard. Saying "Yes to Christ," only requires a prayer of faith and a commitment to that truth.

The Final Question

In that prayer you merely need to render your life to this truth from the Holy Bible.

- (Romans 10:9) If you declare with your mouth, "Jesus is Lord," and believe in your heart that God raised him from the dead, you will be saved.

If you say yes to Jesus, then you have a Savior without end. If not, you will stand alone, a sinner on your own merit, in front of the creator of the universe. Have you received the warnings and petitons from the Lord, or do you wish to go on with the consequence of a forever sin-filled life without grace?

Obviously, God believes in our importance. There should be no squabble and no worthwhile argument, negotiation, or compromise; there is no dialogue to pursue, just the request for forgiveness through the shed blood of the lamb and confessing that Christ is the solitary true redemption. So, in actuality, the final question can be answered now and forever. Do you want Jesus alone as your Savior, or do you want to continue to be without one?

The Lord believes we are worth another try; the response to salvation is the key to everlasting life. If you truly wish to be with God, do I hear an Amen?

Working References

(CARM) Christian Apologetics & Research Ministry
https://carm.org/apologetics

Watchman Fellowship (Christian Apologetics Organization)
http://www.watchman.org/
(Modern-day Idolatry)

Bible Gateway
https://www.biblegateway.com/resources/dictionary-of-bible-themes/8747-false-gods

https://www.biblegateway.com/passage/ (passage lookup)

Wikipedia
https://www.wikipedia.org/
https://search.yahoo.com/yhs/search?p=wikipedia+mt+rush

https://en.wikipedia.org/wiki/World_War_I_casualties

https://en.wikipedia.org/wiki/Timeline_for_the_day_of_the_September_11_attacks

Forbes

www.forbes.com/ … /the-best-and-worst-paying-jobs

About the Author

Greg grew up in his youth hearing about Jesus. However, he met Christ on a personal level at college, and a rebirth of grace was begun. Greg's life as a Villanova graduate English Major and Career as Storage Management professional have been a great blessing. His Christian study, evangelical pursuits, and concentrated theological study span three decades. He still hopes to complete his Christian education through programs with Berean University or in Network study at London University. This is a fertile hope that looms larger now that his girls have mostly completed their undergraduate and graduate careers.

His church life as Board member to one church, Deacon to another, Senior Royal Ranger Commander, Clear Gospel Campaign officer, Choir and Worship leader, and partisan to several national and international missions has given him a saturated view of the love that God can spread with seeds and service.

His first work, "One Lord, Many Ministries" was a fourteen-year endeavor to provide friends and other readers with an outlook of the many counterfiet paths and theologies across the globe and the magnificent truth in Christ.

This next journey brought Greg to a place of focus for reflection on the *one path* that ends with a face to face encounter with a forgiving God.